Disney in Verse

The Rhyme and Reason
Behind Mickey's World

Colleen Ann Myrhol
and
Chuck Schmidt

Theme Park Press
The Happiest Books on Earth
www.ThemeParkPress.com

Theme Park Press publishes its books in a variety of print and electronic formats. Some content that appears in one format may not appear in another.

Editor: Bob McLain
Layout: Artisanal Text

ISBN 978-1-68390-145-7
Printed in the United States of America

Theme Park Press | www.ThemeParkPress.com
Address queries to bob@themeparkpress.com

Contents

During the summer of 2017, as I was finishing my *Disney's Animal Kingdom: An Unofficial History* book, I decided to open up the final chapter of the book to fans of the park, allowing them to express their thoughts and deep feelings about perhaps the most unique theme park experience ever conceived. It was Janet who suggested that it might be a nice touch to mix in a few of Colleen's poems in the chapter. I wholeheartedly agreed.

During our correspondences, it was clear that Colleen had amassed a treasure trove of poems about Disney, everything from poems about the theme parks in general, to individual shows and attractions, to the Disney Vacation Club, the Disney Cruise Line, and the Disney Springs shopping and entertainment district. Again, it was Janet who knew of Colleen's desire to have her poems published and floated the idea of submitting a book proposal to Bob McLain at Theme Park Press, using Colleen's Disney-themed poems as the backbone of the book. I would add a few paragraphs following each poem to give her subject matter some historical perspective and context. Bob loved the idea...and you're holding the result in your hands.

Imagine that: two people who attended the same high school, but never knew each other, meeting for the first time on a Disney cruise on the Mediterranean Sea decades later, then collaborating on a book about a subject they've loved since they were youngsters. Talk about the magic of Disney!

Well-Versed About Disney

We know a lot of goofy things about Disney,
Like the very best places to view a pixie.
Because we both really like poetry and rhyme,
A book combining Disney and verse is about time.
Our book has been titled Disney in Verse,
With hints like if you enter early to go in reverse.

If you are lost, we'll tell you where to meet,
And if you are hungry, we'll suggest places to eat.

Disney has many terrific places to stay,
And they'll be discussed here in a poetic way.

If you're planning your vacation and it's your very first,
Or your ninety-ninth, bring a copy of Disney in Verse.

Wishing

Last night, I was wishing upon a star,
To teach you about Disney wherever you are.

I'll tell you about Mickey, Minnie, and Goofy,
And where to have dinner with Sleeping Beauty.

I'll teach you about Hidden Mickeys and where to look,
All I know about Disney is somewhere inside this book.

One last thing: We'd like to dedicate this book to the late Marty Sklar, the former head of Walt Disney Imagineering, who passed away in July of 2017. Marty had a profound effect on so many people, both Disney cast members and Disney geeks like us. He was a giant in his field, yet was always a humble, caring, and generous soul. He is sorely missed.

CHAPTER ONE

The Magic Kingdom

Celebrating a Magical Place

The Magic Kingdom is something you've never seen before,
It's like entering your imagination through a magical door.

You can ride monorails, pirate boats, and rocket ships,
Eat organically grown salads, or fish and chips.

Travel to a fantasy land on an old-fashioned train,
Sing with colorful Tiki birds about a loud tropical rain.

Spend all of your time allowing your vacation to run wild,
There is no better place for an adult to become a child.

The Kingdom

Special postmarks on your mail,
Delicious candy weighed on a scale.

Casey's hot dogs and ginger ale,
Freshly made popcorn sold by the pail.

A Tiki bird proudly sways its tail,
A puppy watches pirates stuck in a jail.

Riding upon an old-fashioned rail,
Having fun with Chip and Dale.

A pixie as big as your fingernail,
A magical holiday without fail.

Traveling to Walt Disney World

It would be wonderful to take an airline flight,
From any airport, day or night.

It would be magical to sail there upon the sea,
That would certainly be alright with me.

How nice it would be to rent a great big bus,
That would have enough room to hold all of us.

It would be a fantasy to ride in a railroad car,
Or to look out the windows of our family car.

No matter how you arrive at Walt Disney World,
Be totally amazed at the surprises to be unfurled.

Wishing Upon a Star

Dreams take unstoppable determination,
Achieving goals never simply happen.

No matter what obstacles you face,
Never stop pursuing your passion.

Work earnestly toward your endeavors,
With courage, resolve, and compassion.

THE EVOLUTION OF THE MAGIC KINGDOM

Walt Disney never cared about making sequels to his movies. His philosophy was to never look back and live off past successes, but rather, to always look ahead and keep coming up with new and fresh ideas. But the idea of creating a second Disneyland did appeal to him. He realized that Disneyland, which opened on July 17, 1955, in Anaheim, California, was primarily a West Coast phenomenon and that few people east of the Mississippi River had either the means or desire to venture all the way out to the Golden State to visit his first-of-its-kind, family-oriented theme park. And as difficult as it is to believe now, with 12 Disney parks located around the world, adding to Disney's doubts were suspicions that his brand of West Coast entertainment would even be popular on the East Coast.

The success of Disneyland piqued the interest of business concerns. "At first, Walt said there'd never be another Disneyland," Disney executive Donn Tatum said, "but in the late 1950s, he began getting invitations from all over the country and all over the world" to build a Disneyland sequel. One such inquiry came from a group of businessmen from St. Louis, Missouri, which Disney took very seriously. After several months of feasibility studies, "some key person backed out," according to Disney Imagineer John Hench, and the plan to build a Disney park in the Midwest was scrapped.

During the early 1960s, Disney committed his staff to creating four attractions for the 1964–1965 New York World's Fair. These shows—the Magic Skyway in the Ford Motor Company pavilion; Great Moments with Mr. Lincoln at the Illinois state pavilion; "it's a small world," sponsored by Pepsi-Cola; and the Carousel of Progress in the General Electric pavilion—would serve as the ultimate litmus test for Disney entertainment on the East Coast. To paraphrase Frank Sinatra, if the Disney's shows could make it in New York, they could make it anywhere. The four shows were a huge success, proving conclusively that Disney's West Coast brand of entertainment would be successful east of the Mississippi.

While preparing for the World's Fair, Disney committed to making the move east—specifically, to central Florida—which had the type of year-round weather conducive to a vacation destination resort. He secretly sent several of his trusted advisors to the Orlando area, where they purchased tens of thousands of acres of land under the guise of dummy corporations. The game plan was to not only create a sequel to Disneyland, but to construct a utopian city of the future as well. Walt's desire to build an experimental prototype community of tomorrow was "by far... the heart of everything we'll be doing in Disney World."

But when Walt died in 1966, plans for Epcot were put on hold. It was decided that opening the Magic Kingdom theme park—and establishing a sort of beachhead for Disney entertainment on the East Coast, as well as the world's first year-round destination resort—would be the priority.

The Magic Kingdom at Walt Disney World opened on Oct. 1, 1971, and in many ways, the park mirrored the Magic Kingdom at Disneyland: a train station at the entrance; a town square; a Main Street with a fairytale castle in the distance; and a hub area leading to various themed lands. A staff of 5,000 cast members greeted a surprisingly small crowd of 10,000 guests when WDW swung open its gates for the first time. Opening day staples in the park included the now-shuttered Mike Fink Keelboats, Snow White's Adventures, Mr. Toad's Wild Ride, the Mickey Mouse Revue, 20,000 Leagues Under the Sea, and If You Had Wings. Although the park got off to a slow start, by Thanksgiving weekend word had gotten out and Disney World quickly became the country's No. 1 travel destination, a position it has held ever since.

In the years since the Magic Kingdom opened, Disney has added three more theme parks, two water parks, numerous resorts, and a shopping/dining/entertainment district to its Florida property, proving conclusively that Walt Disney's instincts were on the mark when it came to this particular sequel.

Space Mountain

Have you ever gone for a ride through outer space?
Because I know a very special place,
Where you can almost touch the stars,
As you ride through the heavens in tiny red cars.
You'll feel the excitement as your heart starts to race,
On a roller-coaster ride through outer space.

OMG

Space Mountain is not for the faint of heart,
It's a roller coaster that runs in the dark.

A serpentine track of highs and lows,
Through a galaxy where wild energy flows.
Your heart, legs, and neck should be strong,
It may not be the ride to take Grandma along.

SPACE MOUNTAIN'S DELAYED LAUNCH

At a "dinner and a conversation" event in 2011, former Imagineering president Marty Sklar told several insightful stories about the Walt Disney Company and a few of its prominent cast members. But Marty saved the best for last with what he called "my Space Mountain story."

The original concept for Space Mountain was created by Sklar's mentor, John Hench, way back in 1965. There was one problem: "Computer technology wasn't sophisticated enough back then to bring it to life," Sklar said.

In the late 1960s, following the success of the Matterhorn Bobsleds attraction, the RCA company offered Disney $10 million to come up with a roller-coaster-type attraction to be placed in Tomorrowland in Disneyland. "We worked nine months on a concept and we thought it was great," Sklar said. "It was based on a trip inside a computer."

Marty and his team were asked to make a pitch to RCA at its headquarters in Manhattan. "We brought in seven large storyboards. They took up most of the wall, but many of the drawings were small. RCA's president [David Sarnoff] always sat in the same seat at the end of the table. I knew there was no way he could see the storyboards from where he was sitting. We asked the RCA people if Sarnoff could sit closer to the storyboards, but they told us 'Mr. Sarnoff always sits at the head of the table.'

"We made the presentation and I saw Sarnoff scribble something down on a piece of paper. He handed it to the guy sitting next to him, and he passed it down the table. It got down to me and I opened it up. It said, 'Who are these guys?' No one had explained to him who we were and why we were there. We went back to California and I told my boss, 'I don't care if you fire me. I'm not going back there.'

"'But Marty,' he said, 'there's 10 million dollars on the table. You have to do it.'" By now, John Hench's original roller-coaster idea had become feasible, so Sklar and his team returned to Manhattan months later with a new ride concept—a space-themed roller-coaster in the dark—along with new storyboards and a new strategy in hand.

"We made sure Mr. Sarnoff sat in the middle of the table. When someone asked him why he always sat at the end of the table, he said, 'Because no one ever asked me to sit anywhere else.'"

With RCA's financial backing in hand, Walt Disney Imagineering went about the task of bringing Space Mountain from concept to reality. But with the success of the Magic Kingdom at Walt Disney World, Disney's higher-ups decided that Space Mountain would be better served as WDW's first major thrill ride. The placement of a space-themed attraction in Florida also made perfect sense, since NASA's launch facility was located just 60 minutes due east of Orlando at Cape Canaveral.

Four years after the Magic Kingdom opened in Florida, Space Mountain debuted, on Jan. 15, 1975, with the usual pomp, ceremony...and a few NASA astronauts in attendance.

Since opening in 1975, Space Mountain has been the top thrill ride in the Magic Kingdom. Similar Space Mountains, though not exact replicas, are located in all of Disney's Magic Kingdom-style parks, save for Shanghai Disneyland, which has a unique roller-coaster of its own, known as the Tron Lightcycles (a Tron Lightcycle attraction is now in the planning stages for Walt Disney World, to be built adjacent to Space Mountain).

Throughout the years, Space Mountain has been upgraded to reflect advancements in roller-coaster technology. There also have been changes to the queue and

post-show experiences. Though they appear to be travel-
ing much faster, Space Mountain's ride vehicles reach a top
speed of 28 mph; they take 2½ minutes to careen on a track
that's 4,000 feet long, through the darkened expanse of
the 183-feet tall, 300-feet wide futuristic building.

Space Mountain brought a true feeling of space travel
to Tomorrowland and represented a quantum leap
forward from the opening day attractions there, which
included the Grand Prix Raceway, Flight to the Moon,
a CircleVision 360 film titled *America the Beautiful*, and If
You Had Wings.

Lighting the Night Along Main Street U.S.A.

A magical parade of sparkling lights and sounds,
Of fairytale characters and brightly colored clowns.

I try to get as close as possible, so I can see
The night-time wonders Disney has created for me.

As Snow White passes, she regally waves all around,
Followed by Cinderella dressed in a brilliant blue gown.

It's so wonderful to watch a glittering night-time parade,
The parade may end, but my memories will never fade.

FLIPPING THE SWITCH ON THE MAIN STREET ELECTRICAL PARADE

A few months after Walt Disney World opened in 1971,
Disney's higher-ups explored the possibility of adding a
night-time show to its entertainment mix. The plan was
to give guests leaving the park a "kiss goodnight" in the
form of a light and music show on the Seven Seas Lagoon
and Bay Lake.

Disney's Imagineers came up with a concept for what
they called the Electrical Water Pageant, which would
feature thousands of twinkling lights affixed to aluminum
wire mesh forms of dolphins, dragons, and fish. Those

forms were bolted to a string of 10 30-feet long pontoon boats. On board the pontoons were gigantic speakers which pumped out Disney-themed music and patriotic tunes. The show could be seen from the boat loading docks at the Magic Kingdom, as well as from the beachfronts of the Contemporary and Polynesian resorts. The Electrical Water Pageant was an immediate hit, spurring Disney's planners to devise a similar show for landlubbers.

After noting the popularity of the Electrical Water Pageant, Disney CEO Card Walker wanted to offer Disneyland guests a similar night-time experience. Bob Jani and project director Ron Miziker came up with the Main Street Electrical Parade, which has become one of the most beloved, innovative shows in Disney parks history.

The Main Street Electrical Parade debuted on June 17, 1972, at the Magic Kingdom in Disneyland. It featured a string of individual parade floats, each decorated with thousands of twinkling light bulbs, all themed to a classic Disney movie, with most of the floats carrying characters from those movies. Each float was powered by 500 nickel-cadmium batteries. In addition to the floats, which sported a total of 500,000 lights, there were dozens of costumed cast members—also bedecked in a total of 11,000 lights—walking or dancing alongside. What made the parade so innovative was a synchronized soundtrack (to the heavily synthesized song "Baroque Hoedown") which played in conjunction with the on-board lights.

Key to the success of the parade was the creation of radio-activated "trigger zones." Since the series of parade floats stretched for more than 2,000 feet, Disney's planners devised a system where the soundtrack would be played as each float entered into a zone, enabling guests to hear music specific to the float nearest to them through the park's audio system. The zone system allowed for each guest to experience the same show, no matter where they were stationed along Main Street.

Disneyland's version of the Main Street Electrical Parade was so popular that a similar version debuted on June 11, 1977, at the Magic Kingdom in Walt Disney World. Various iterations of the parade have been shown at Disneyland Paris, Tokyo Disneyland, and Disney California Adventure. Over the years, Disney switched out the Main Street Electrical Parade with SpectroMagic, a similar presentation with newer floats and a different soundtrack. It's even been renamed, to just Disney's Electrical Parade. In addition, there have been nighttime parades with twinkling lights, themed floats, music, and costumed characters during the Halloween and Christmas seasons, as well as versions known as Paint the Night and Light Magic.

The Main Street Electrical Parade was revived in early 2017 in Walt Disney World and ran until August of the same year before riding off into the moonlight for presumably the last time.

Cinderella Castle

What could be more romantic than a castle with a view,
Painted colors of tranquil skies, soft white and powder blue?
The palace walls within are covered with tiles of shiny gold,
It's the finest place on Earth where fairy tales were ever told.
The castle spires reach as high as heaven's stars and the moon
The only compensation of leaving is knowing you'll be back soon.

A FAIRYTALE PALACE COMES TO LIFE

The evolution of Disney's iconic castles is as fascinating as the fairytales on which they are based.

It all started, of course, with Sleeping Beauty Castle in Disneyland, which debuted in 1955 along with the rest of the park. To those first Disneyland guests, the naming of the castle to honor Sleeping Beauty may have seemed a bit curious—the Disney movie of the same name, which followed the trials and tribulations of the princess Aurora, wouldn't be released until 1959.

Still, those guests fell in love with the dreamy, romantic nature of the castle, which seemed to be lifted from some far-off European landscape and transplanted to southern California. The design of Sleepy Beauty Castle took its inspiration from many castles, both real and in classic literature. Still, key elements from the Neuschwanstein Castle in Bavaria, Germany, seem to be most prevalent in Disneyland's castle.

Sleeping Beauty Castle stands 75 feet tall, making it the shortest Disney castle of them all. One key feature that differentiates it from the other Disney castles is the fact that inside Sleeping Beauty Castle there's a walk-through attraction, which includes dioramas and CGI technology that present the detailed story of Sleeping Beauty. The original walk-through debuted in 1957, with dioramas based on the work of artist Eyvind Earle. It closed in 2001, much to the chagrin of former Disney Imagineer Tony Baxter, who then championed for its return. He dug through the company's archives in an attempt to both replicate and upgrade the original. "It was like an archaeology expedition trying to piece it back together," Baxter said. "We had a few drawings and one ViewMaster 3-D picture" to work with. The new, high-tech Sleeping Beauty Castle walk-through debuted on November 27, 2008, and has been a hit ever since.

When the Magic Kingdom in Walt Disney World opened in 1971, its castle—named after Disney princess Cinderella—could be seen from miles away. That's because, at 189 feet, it was more than 100 feet taller than Sleeping Beauty Castle. And Disney's designers used an old movie trick, called forced perspective, to make it seem even taller. Keeping in mind that Florida can be hit with powerful hurricanes, Cinderella Castle was built to be able to withstand winds of 110 mph. There are 27 towers on the castle, a large clock, and, if you look closely, there are 13 gargoyles positioned on its balconies. There are five murals located in the castle's walkway consisting of more than 1 million pieces of Italian glass tile. The murals, each 15 x 10 feet in dimension, took 22 months to complete. In 1996, to celebrate Walt Disney World's 25th anniversary on October 1, Cinderella Castle was transformed into a giant birthday cake. More than 200 gallons of pink paint was used to turn the edifice into a giant confection. In addition, 26 candles, 16 candy stars, 16 candy bears, 12 gumdrops, 4 Life Savers, 30 lollipops, and 50 gumballs were affixed to the outside of the structure. The decorations were removed on January 31, 1998, and Cinderella Castle was repainted to its original color.

The original design for Cinderella Castle called for an apartment to be built where Walt Disney and his family could stay. Walt died before the park opened and the apartment space sat dormant for decades. In 2006, the would-be apartment was turned into a fantasy suite where lucky guests could spend the night. The suite features gold-inlaid tile, a bath tub with shimmering stars embedded in the ceiling, and a "magic mirror" that turns into a television.

Every Magic Kingdom-style Disney park features a castle. Hong Kong Disneyland's castle most closely resembles Disneyland's in style and size. Tokyo Disneyland's Cinderella Castle is similar to Walt Disney World's, while the newest and largest castle in Shanghai Disneyland, known as Enchanted Storybook Castle, has a boat attraction (Voyage to the Crystal Grotto) that runs under it. Disneyland Paris' castle—Le Chateau de la Belle au Bois Dormant—has a feature that is both unique and unexpected: a giant dragon. "I thought if there's one thing I could do to distinguish this castle from any other castle you're going to visit in Europe or in France," Baxter said, "it would be to deliver on the dream of dragons living in the bowels of the castle."

In addition to serving as each park's icon, the Disney castles are used as the focal point of night-time projection shows, adding even more grandeur to structures that have come to epitomize Disney charm and creativity.

The Haunted Mansion

There's a very scary place
Full of goblins and ghouls.
It's the Haunted Mansion
And inside there are no rules.

So be extra careful
If you decide to go inside,
Because there is absolutely
No safe place to hide!

A PLACE WHERE GRIM, GRINNING GHOSTS COME OUT TO SOCIALIZE

The Haunted Mansion was the final piece of the New Orleans expansion in Disneyland, which played out over several years. The new land, located on the banks of the Rivers of America, was dedicated in July of 1966, a few months before Walt Disney's death. The land took its inspiration from classic New Orleans architecture, complete with elaborate wrought-iron fencing. In March 1967, the Pirates of the Caribbean boat ride opened, giving New Orleans Square a signature E-ticket attraction. A heavily themed restaurant, the Blue Bayou, also opened in conjunction with the Pirates attraction. Then, in May of 1967, Club 33, an exclusive VIP lounge, was added to the New Orleans Square mix.

All the while, a daunting, haunting, antebellum mansion had stood unoccupied near New Orleans Square since 1963. In fact, as far back as 1961 the Haunted Mansion was listed as a "coming attraction" on park handbills and on signs posted outside the mansion. Although the plans for the building went through many different iterations, Walt's basic premise—to create an off-beat, "museum of the weird" attraction—held true throughout the years. A variety of Disney designers, including Harper Goff, Ken Anderson, Rolly Crump, and Yale Gracey, took stabs at creating a storyline for the attraction, with many different themes growing in and out of favor.

Disney's involvement in the 1964–1965 New York World's Fair, the repositioning of the four Disney-created fair attractions to Disneyland, as well as the secret development of Walt Disney World in Florida, put plans for Disneyland's Haunted Mansion on hold. Walt's death also stalled the project that he had championed for years. When plans for the Haunted Mansion were revived in 1967, Imagineers Claude Coats, X Atencio, and Marc Davis made key contributions as development of the attraction began to take shape. The advancements made with Audio-Animatronics figures during the New York World's Fair also added a key component to the Haunted Mansion's storyline.

Initially, a restaurant was proposed for the attraction (similar to the Blue Bayou near Pirates of the Caribbean), but that idea was nixed. In addition, the attraction was planned to be a walk-through, giving it a museum-like, though low-capacity, element. The development of another Disney theme park staple—the Omnimover ride system—enabled Disney to be able to move guests quickly and decidedly more efficiently through the attraction. The Omnimover's continuous chain of ride vehicles, dubbed Doom Buggies, carried guests into a series of rooms and elaborate ghostly tableaus, where 999 "grim, grinning ghosts come out the socialize." One scene features the head of a ghost, encased in a crystal ball, talking to guests. The ghost's head was modeled after Leota Toombs, a former member of WED Enterprises, the forerunner of Walt Disney Imagineering. Another classic scene takes place in a dining room where "ghosts" dance around an elongated table adorned with candelabra and dishes placed in the shape of Mickey Mouse heads.

In keeping with the mansion's lighthearted nature, Disney's creative staff had the opportunity to poke fun at themselves, particularly on the faces of the tombstones outside the attraction.

When the Haunted Mansion finally opened in Disneyland on August 9, 1969, it did so to rave reviews. Although it is considered a dark ride and has several scenes that might be too intense for younger guests, the attraction is more fun than frightful. Similar versions of the Haunted Mansion are located in the Magic Kingdoms at Walt Disney World (in Liberty Square) and Tokyo Disneyland (in Fantasyland). There is a Mystic Manor (located in Mystic Point) in Hong Kong Disneyland and a Phantom Manor in Disneyland Paris (in Frontierland).

Since 2001, the Haunted Mansion at Disneyland has been transformed into the Haunted Mansion Holiday during the Halloween and Christmas seasons, featuring scenes, characters, and themes from Tim Burton's *The Nightmare Before Christmas*, a cult classic that was released in 1993. The attraction culminates with the graveyard scene covered in realistic-looking snow.

"it's a small world"

I've often heard the phrase, it's a small world,
And I'll assure you that statement is true.
The first time we sailed on it's a small world,
I fell in love with its melody...and with you.
A lot has changed since that April day in 1964,
But every time we take that ride, I love you even more.

A DISNEY ATTRACTION THAT
SPEAKS TO PEACE AND HARMONY

"There's just one moon and one golden sun, and a smile means friendship to everyone." Those words were written for the "it's a small world" attraction by Disney composers Richard and Robert Sherman. "Imagine," said former Imagineering executive Marty Sklar, "what a wonderful world this would be if we all went along with those words."

"it's a small world" was one of four attractions developed by Disney's creative staff for the 1964–1965 New York World's Fair. It was sponsored by the Pepsi-Cola Company, with proceeds (the ride had a separate admission price) going to the United Nations International Children's Emergency Fund (UNICEF).

Walt Disney had already committed to designing three shows for the fair when he was convinced to add a fourth attraction just 11 months before the international exposition was scheduled to open. "Starting that attraction 11 months from opening day was kind of nuts, it really was," Sklar said. "But it shows you how smart the mechanical people are. They made everything simple, taking things right off the shelves at the studio."

From the outset, "it's a small world"—dubbed the happiest cruise that ever sailed—was to be a boat ride through the different lands of seven continents, with hundreds of colorfully dressed dolls representing residents of those countries.

The Sherman Brothers' song, written as a roundelay, is among the attraction's most endearing features. Along with the distinctive round-faced dolls—created by artist Mary Blair, known for her distinctive color stylings—it gives "it's a small world" its enduring appeal. The dolls, each three-feet tall, are dressed in authentic costumes designed by Disney animator Marc Davis and his wife, Alice Davis.

Disney's creative team, in conjunction with amusement park ride builder Arrow Development, came up with a boat-ride concept for the attraction, where flat-bottom boats would be gently pushed by water jets through a continuous trough filled with water. The success of "it's a small world" allowed Disney's designers to turn the planned walk-through version of Pirates of the Caribbean into a more realistic boat ride.

The Small World vessels were originally called FantaSea boats—a play on the word "fantasy"—but when Disney and sponsor Pepsi-Cola realized that Fanta was a subsidiary of Coca-Cola, Pepsi's biggest rival, the name was dropped.

According to Frank Stanek, former senior planner at Walt Disney Imagineering who worked extensively on "it's a small world," the pavilion which housed the attraction also featured two refreshment stands. "Early on, the pavilion had two drink bars serving Pepsi-Cola at the entrance of the attraction. We found that the visitors were also looking for something to eat as well, so at some point during the first season, we expanded the counter service to include prepared sandwiches and chips on the menu."

After the fair closed in the fall of 1965, "it's a small world"—dolls, props, boats, and even the water troughs— were trucked back to Disneyland, where a new building had been constructed to house the attraction in the Fantasyland section of the park. The attraction's loading and unloading area is located outside the pavilion. In addition, the Walt Disney World Railroad runs behind the building's façade.

One highly visible feature of the "it's a small world" fair attraction, located outside the building—the prominent Tower of the Four Winds, created by Rolly Crump—did not make it back to California. To this day, the whereabouts of the kinetic panel structure remain a mystery.

"it's a small world" was one of the featured attractions when Walt Disney World opened in 1971. It remains one of the Magic Kingdom's most iconic attractions. Similar versions are featured in the other Magic Kingdoms around the world.

Wings

As the guest of Eastern Airlines
And, of course, Walt Disney, too,
You could have flown to any destination
That seemed appealing to you.
You could have tanned on a sunny beach,
Or climbed mountains covered with snow.
If You Had Wings could have flown you
To anywhere you wanted to go.

IF YOU HAD WINGS WAS A MAGIC KINGDOM ORIGINAL

When you look closely at an aerial view of the Magic Kingdom in Walt Disney World, you'll notice something interesting: attractions are a lot bigger than they appear to be when you're standing outside at the entrance—and not only that, but each building you see from above more often than not houses more than one attraction. Take the building in Tomorrowland, which is home to both Buzz Lightyear's Space Ranger Spin and Monsters Inc. Laugh Floor: one building, two attractions.

Shortly after the Magic Kingdom opened in 1971, that building was home to two completely different attractions: the CircleVision 360 film *America the Beautiful* played in the section now occupied by Monsters Inc., while If You Had Wings (which officially opened in June of 1972) was the main draw where Buzz Lightyear now holds sway.

If You Had Wings was considered a "dark ride," even though the main goal of the attraction was to feature the sunny destinations of the ride's sponsor, Eastern Airlines. The attraction put guests in two-person vehicles attached to an Omnimover ride system, which moved the vehicles continuously through the four-minute-plus attraction. The Omnimover system allowed the vehicles to spin and travel up and down inclines along the track.

The ride featured a catchy theme song written by Disney composer Buddy Baker and lyricist X Atencio.

If You Had Wings was unique to the Magic Kingdom during its run because it did not require a pre-paid ticket. When the park first opened, guests paid a general admission fee to enter the park, then needed to present a coupon to ride each attraction. The attractions were graded in terms of their thrill level. For example, the placid Main Street vehicles required an A-ticket, which cost 10 cents, while the most thrilling adventures in the park (at the time, Jungle Cruise, Haunted Mansion, and the Hall of Presidents were judged the most exciting) needed E-tickets, which cost 90 cents. If You Had Wings, America the Beautiful, and the Diamond Horseshoe Revue were the only free attractions in the park.

If You Had Wings afforded guests the opportunity to "travel" to the Caribbean, ancient Mexico, New Orleans, Bermuda, and other exciting ports of call that were serviced by Eastern Airlines. One memorable scene showed the first-class cabin of an airliner, where an elaborate table setting awaited hungry passengers. There also was a scene where a police officer in the Bahamas directed traffic, signaling that it was safe for pedestrians, autos—and a flock of flamingos—to cross the intersection. The ride culminated with the voice of actor Orson Welles telling riders: "You *do* have wings. You *can* do all these things. You *can* widen your world. Eastern: the wings of man."

When Eastern Airlines filed for bankruptcy in the late 1980s, Delta Airlines became the official airline of Walt Disney World and took over sponsorship of the pavilion, offering its own version of the attraction, titled Delta Dreamflight. It used the same track, but updated the show scenes and musical score. The attraction went through two non-sponsored iterations (If You Could Fly and Take Flight) before it closed for good in 1996, to be replaced by Buzz Lightyear's Space Ranger Spin.

Main Street, U.S.A.

Browsing along Main Street makes shopping a pleasure,
There's everything you need to create a family treasure.

A personalized Mickey hat, or a Minnie framed silhouette,
You can even find an embroidered Pluto jacket for your pet.

Pick up some CD recordings of your favorite Disney music,
I suggest "The Lion King" melodies, they are very therapeutic.

The bank is open whenever Disney guests are present,
And gift cards are always perfect for every adolescent.

The stationery store has fabulous cards and pens,
Oh, one more thing: don't forget postcards for your friends.

THE MAGIC KINGDOM'S MAIN DRAG

Walt Disney was a son of the Midwest. Though born in Chicago in 1901, his family moved to quaint Marceline, Missouri, when he was 5, and he grew up on a farm, where he began to show an interest in drawing. In 1911, the Disneys moved to Kansas City where Walt became enamored with amusement parks, vaudeville, and motion pictures—interests that would stay with him for the rest of his life.

When plans were being drawn up for Disneyland in the early 1950s, Walt conceptualized a thoroughfare near the entrance of the park that would embody an idealized town at the turn of the 20th century—similar to the type of Midwestern town he grew up in or visited while delivering newspapers. Although Main Street, U.S.A., isn't modeled after any one town in particular, Marceline is widely recognized as the place that Walt used for inspiration in creating the park's main roadway.

At the time of Disneyland's conceptualization, the Walt Disney Company was primarily a movie company. In keeping with moviemakers' tenet of creating a strong opening scene, Main Street provided guests with such a table-setter: a friendly, home-spun environment that portended of exciting adventures ahead.

Disneyland's Main Street was built using another standard movie technique: forced perspective. The ground floors of all the buildings along the street were built at about 7/8th scale, with the floors above getting gradually smaller. The use of forced perspective allowed for the buildings to appear to be taller than they really are.

Just like the real main avenues in America's small towns, Main Street in Disneyland provided ample opportunity for guests to shop and eat. Indeed, Disneyland's shops were designed to be interconnected. Although the façades outside gave the impression there were many different stores along Main Street, guests could enter one of the stores, in particular the Emporium, and meander from one end of the street down to the other. The idea of enclosed, interconnected shops made Main Street, in essence, the world's first indoor shopping mall.

When guests arrive at Disneyland (or Walt Disney World or Disneyland Paris or Hong Kong Disneyland) they walk under the train station and into Town Square, which is actually a circular area where a flag pole sits center stage (the main thoroughfare in Tokyo Disneyland is called World Bazaar and is covered, while the newest entry street in Shanghai Disneyland is known as Mickey Avenue and is inspired by many of Disney's animated stars). To the left in the parks with Main Streets is City Hall, which serves as a guest relations center. Main Street begins where Town Square ends, with spectacular views of a storybook castle up ahead. Most of the Main Streets in Disney's Magic Kingdom-style parks also feature vehicles—either motorized or horse-drawn—that regularly traverse up and down the street.

Another Main Street staple in Disney parks are windows that honor the men and women who helped create each park. There are a few exceptions, of course. For instance, there's a window in Disneyland dedicated to Elias Disney, Walt's father, above the Emporium. There are even windows located off-Main Street. In Frontierland, near the Golden Horseshoe, a window is dedicated to Fess Parker, TV's Davy Crockett, the fabled "king of the wild frontier," who helped dedicate the land when the park opened on July 17, 1955.

Off We Go!

Heigh-ho, heigh-ho, and off we go,
On a ride where bright jewels glow.
Speeding by on a runaway cart,
A glorious adventure from the very start.
Tracks with tall heights and depths that are low,
A secret canyon that only a few actually know.

THE LONG AND WINDING JOURNEY OF THE SEVEN DWARFS MINE TRAIN

It was a long and winding journey for the Seven Dwarfs Mine Train roller-coaster, one that saw it go from off to on like a light switch during the planning stages for the new Fantasyland expansion in the Magic Kingdom at Walt Disney World.

The announcement for the monumental Fantasyland overhaul came in September of 2009, when Parks and Resorts chairman Jay Rasulo broke the news at the annual D23 convention. The original plans for new Fantasyland included a Pixie Hollow area, similar but larger in scope to the Pixie area in Disneyland. But there was no Seven Dwarfs Mine Train in those preliminary plans.

Inside Pixie Hollow were areas earmarked for Cinderella- and Aurora-themed attractions. The heavy princess theming was due in part to the immense popularity of the lucrative stable of Disney princesses.

But then Pixie Hollow was abruptly scrapped in 2011— reportedly because the next Disney Parks and Resorts chairman, Tom Staggs, thought the new land didn't have enough attractions for boys—adding its name to the long list of announced, but never-built Disney attractions. As Disney's creative team fine-tuned what was called the largest expansion in Magic Kingdom history, its most interesting "tweak" to the master plan was the addition of the Seven Dwarfs Mine Train coaster ride in the middle of the Fantasyland expansion.

Snow White, of course, had had a strong presence in WDW's Magic Kingdom with the Snow White's Scary Adventures attraction, a Fantasyland staple since 1971. As part of the expansion, that attraction was scrapped in favor of Princess Fairytale Hall, an elaborate meet-and-greet area for princess aficionados. Rather than have Ms. White and her seven vertically challenged cohorts fade into Disney parks lore, Snow and the boys resurfaced as the stars of the Seven Dwarfs Mine Train coaster.

Actual construction of New Fantasyland began in early 2010 on the section of the park that once was home to the 20,000 Leagues Under the Sea adventure.

New Fantasyland opened in stages. Imagineer Diego Parras said in 2012: "Since new Fantasyland will be so massive, we opted to open it in phases to get the experience to guests as quickly as possible."

The new land—featuring Under the Sea ~ Journey of the Little Mermaid and Enchanted Tales with Belle—saw its official grand opening in December 2012. The mine Train began rolling over, under, around, and through the diamond mine the following spring.

The Seven Dwarfs Mine Train features a new ride system—the ride vehicles have the ability to sway back and forth while hurtling along the tubular steel track. The vehicles look like actual wooden mining ore buckets. Animated figures of Snow White and the Seven Dwarfs, as well as music from the classic animated film, appear during the train's trek into the diamond mine and at ride's end. Since this attraction is located in Fantasyland, it's thrilling, but still family-friendly.

In keeping with Disney's new philosophy on lines, there's an interactive queue available to stand-by guests prior to boarding the mine train.

Magic Kingdom's Carousels

As soon as I saw the carousel, I immediately felt at home,
Because I remember the day my parents let me ride it alone.

The craftsmanship is certain, though some colors have changed,
And a few of the horses on the carousel have been rearranged.

But one thing is certain: it is the same carousel, for sure,
So, if you are feeling sad, a ride would certainly be a cure.

IT MAY HAVE ALL
STARTED WITH A CAROUSEL

When historians look back at the genesis of the Walt Disney Company's entry into the theme park business, they needn't look past Walt's love of trains and his insistence that there be a place where parents and children could have fun together.

"Saturday was always 'Daddy's Day' with the two daughters," Walt often said, meaning that on many Saturdays, Walt would take daughters Sharon and Diane to an amusement park, where they'd run around, burn off steam, and then hop on a carousel. Walt would dutifully sit and watch from a nearby bench as the girls spun round and round atop their wooden chargers.

Years later, when Walt committed his company to building Disneyland, his wife Lillian was opposed to her husband getting involved with anything that resembled the sleazy, tawdry amusement parks of the day. "My park will be different," Walt assured his wife, and then he went about designing a place where families could share in the fun and excitement together in a clean, friendly environment.

When Disneyland was in the planning stages, a traditional carousel was included in the plans.

The King Arthur Carrousel has been the centerpiece of Fantasyland since Disneyland opened in 1955. Since money was tight in the months leading up to Disneyland's debut, wooden horses from shuttered amusement parks around the country were purchased by Disney and shipped to California, where they were meticulously refurbished and placed under the royal canopy.

Over the years, Disneyland's carousel has been updated, but still remains a must-do for families with younger children, even with more advanced and decidedly more high-tech options available elsewhere in the park.

When the Magic Kingdom in Walt Disney World opened in 1971, Cinderella's Golden Carrousel could be seen by guests as they approached the archway of Cinderella Castle leading into Fantasyland; it, too, was the centerpiece of the enchanted land where princesses and princes abound.

Much like Disneyland, WDW's carousel was recycled. It was built in 1917 and was discovered in Olympic Park in Maplewood, New Jersey. Disney's craftsmen refurbished all of the structure's 72 horses and also painted the wooden canopy with scenes from the Disney classic *Cinderella*.

In 2010, Walt Disney World took the unprecedented step of renaming the attraction, and on June 1, it became the Prince Charming Regal Carrousel. Here is the official story behind the name change:

> Following their fairytale romance and happily-ever-after wedding, Cinderella and Prince Charming took up residence in Cinderella Castle. With peace throughout the kingdom, Prince Charming had time to practice for jousting tournaments.
>
> In the countryside near the castle, he built a training device of carved horses, on which he could practice the art of ring-spearing, a tournament event in which a knight rides his horse full speed, lance in hand, toward a small ring hanging from a tree limb, with the object of spearing the ring. This event was known by various

names throughout the lands, but generally came to be called "carrousel."

The carrousel device drew the attention of the villagers, who wanted to take a turn on this amazing spinning contraption. So, Prince Charming had a second carrousel constructed closer to the castle, where everyone could take a spin on this wondrous invention.

Instead of a working knight's training device, however, this new carrousel is more befitting its regal location in the castle courtyard—its rustic training horses replaced with ornately decorated prancing steeds adorned with golden helmets and shields, flower garlands, feathers, and other festoons. Prince Charming invites one and all to test their horsemanship skills and to enjoy their own happy ending.

CHAPTER TWO

Epcot

Epcot

Epcot is a place of faraway lands,
Of pre-Colombian art and marching bands.
You can shop in a Japanese department store,
Or buy a book on old German folklore.
Spend a leisurely hour in Paris, France,
Or, get a Scottish kilt to replace your pants.
You can stop in London for a spot of tea,
Or just enjoy the shade of an animal-shaped tree.
Epcot has so many things to see and do,
There's plenty of fun and adventure for me and you

EPCOT: FROM NAPKIN SKETCH TO A TWO-PRONGED ENTERTAINMENT VENUE

Walt Disney's vision for Epcot was far different than what was eventually opened on October 1, 1982. For one thing, Walt's plan was to overhaul the way American cities were designed. He envisioned an experimental prototype community of tomorrow, where people could live, work, and play without the typical hustle-and-bustle associated with urban areas. It would be a planned and thoughtfully designed community unlike anything that had ever been built before.

Gone would be traffic, pollution, and urban blight so common in many of the metropolises of the 1960s; instead, he planned to start from scratch and offer reliable and clean-running transportation, efficient and Earth-friendly garbage and waste systems, plenty of open space to relax and recreate...a true utopian concept.

Walt drew a rough sketch of his plans for Epcot on a napkin. Once central Florida was chosen as the place where Epcot would be built, plans began to take shape. In October 1966, after the company secretly purchased more than 28,000 acres of land just south of Orlando, Walt recorded a short film, laying out all his hopes and dreams for the so-called Florida Project. Known as the "Epcot Film," Walt went into remarkable detail about what this city of the future would look like and how it would function. There would be a business district at the heart of the circular design, followed by an area with shops, restaurants and entertainment options. The outer rim would have open recreational areas and, finally, housing for the city's residents. The entire city would be climate-controlled, since it would be encased in a giant dome. Transportation within the city would include monorails and PeopleMovers, not fossil-fuel burning automobiles, trucks, and buses.

In December 1966, however, Walt Disney died. Plans for his city of the future were put on hold and the Walt Disney Company shifted gears, going full-speed ahead with building the world's first year-round vacation destination resort, with a Disneyland-style Magic Kingdom theme park serving as its focal point. Walt Disney World opened in October of 1971 with the Magic Kingdom, two resort hotels, a camp ground facility, and a variety of recreational venues.

Once the success of the Magic Kingdom was assured, Disney CEO Card Walker posed this question to Marty Sklar of Walt Disney Imagineering in 1974: "What are we going to do about Epcot?" It took eight years ("It was a pretty fantastic eight years, I must say," Sklar commented), but Epcot finally became a reality in 1982.

However, the original concept for Epcot—an experimental prototype community of tomorrow—was deemed impossible without Walt's guiding hand. Many different ideas were tossed around for a second park in central Florida. In the end, Epcot became a two-pronged project: Future World, which would showcase the nation's technological advances, and World Showcase, which would offer highlights of several different participating countries— sort of a permanent world's fair.

Crucial to the development of the "new" Epcot was getting America's top corporations, as well as companies from around the world, to pony up millions of dollars to sponsor pavilions. "These projects are so expensive," Sklar said. "Without the sponsors, particularly in those days, you couldn't do those kinds of things." In Future World, for instance, many of America's leading businesses anted up millions to have their names associated with Epcot. And in all but one case, World Showcase's pavilions were sponsored by companies from each individual country. The one country not sponsored by a company was Morocco, whose king at the time insisted that his country, and not a company, put up the funds.

When Epcot opened—and, indeed, to this day— young ambassadors for each country served as hosts and hostesses. They're well-versed and knowledgeable representatives of their countries who lend an air of authenticity to each pavilion.

Epcot cost an estimated $1.4 billion to build. During construction, Epcot was the largest building project in the world. More than 3,000 designers worked hand-in-hand with 22 construction companies, which employed an estimated 10,000 workers.

Construction began on October 1, 1979. Although the Epcot that opened on October 1, 1982, was a far cry from Walt's vision for a "community of tomorrow," it was one of the most unique entertainment and educational venues

ever conceived. The park features many distinctive offer-
ings, including its night-time fireworks and laser show
called IllumiNations: Reflections of Earth, which has
been a World Showcase mainstay since 1999. It also holds
seasonal festivals (Festival of the Arts in the winter,
Flower & Garden in the spring, and Food & Wine in the
fall) to enhance its overall presentation.

In 2017, Epcot celebrated its 35th anniversary with
plans in the works to expand, update, or add new attrac-
tions to its already eclectic mix.

No Passport Required

We traveled from London to Mexico,
With a few fantastic stops in between.
We had fish and chips in England,
With nary time to see the queen.
I love Epcot's World Showcase,
With so many places around the globe to roam.
But our vacations are always magical,
Because we call the Disney Vacation Club home.

TAKE A TRIP AROUND THE WORLD IN JUST ONE DAY

The late Charlie Ridgway, who was the press and publicity
director for Walt Disney World from opening day until
his retirement in the mid-1990s, was proud of the fact
that he came up with the idea of calling the buildings
lining Epcot's World Showcase by each country's name,
rather than referring to them as pavilions. He felt that
guests would truly feel as if they were traveling around
the world if, instead of calling it the French pavilion or
the Canada pavilion, they would say, "I'm going to dinner
in France" or "Let's go see the film in Canada." (The one
exception was the American Adventure, since guests
already were in the United States.)

"I had a hand in calling those showcases...by name of the country rather than using the country name as an adjective, as was the practice at most world's fairs," he said.

World Showcase in Epcot is often referred to as a permanent world's fair. There are 11 pavilions rimming the World Showcase Lagoon, representing a mix of countries from Europe, Asia, Africa, and North America. To date, there are no countries representing Central or South America. In the month prior to Epcot's opening in 1982, preview pamphlets hinted at additional countries and/or regions that would be added to the World Showcase mix: Equatorial Africa, Spain, Israel, and the Soviet Union were among the proposed additions to World Showcase. Those pavilions fell through, according to former Imagineering executive Marty Sklar, when they failed to secure corporate sponsorship.

World Showcase went through several design revisions during its early planning stages. One such design would have placed World Showcase around a central courtyard, with each country equally represented in a series of bays, similar to slices of a pie. That idea was scrapped in favor of individual buildings and landscapes that were more representative of each land, all built around a large lagoon. The American Adventure pavilion, for example, is modeled after a Colonial American manor house and is representative of the United States during its early days. Germany takes on the appearance of a biergarten, while France has floral displays and winding streets reminiscent of Paris, complete with a replica of the Eiffel Tower off in the distance.

On opening day, World Showcase consisted of nine pavilions representing Canada, the United Kingdom, France, Japan, the United States, Italy, Germany, China, and Mexico. Morocco was added to the fold in 1984, then in 1988 Norway joined World Showcase, giving it its current complement of 11. Save for Morocco, each World Showcase pavilion receives corporate sponsorship. The pavilions are staffed by cultural representatives, often college students, who hail from each country.

"The big thing we did was the World Showcase fellowship program," Sklar said. "We brought over young people for each pavilion to be the operators of the pavilions there. That was a huge deal. It meant going to Washington and convincing them that we had to have a whole different setup to allow those students to be in the country for a year. At the time, [the program] didn't exist and they worked with us to accomplish that."

All 11 pavilions have restaurants on their properties, serving dishes and delicacies specific to that country, like pizza in Italy, crepes in France, and tacos in Mexico. Importantly, the food is managed by each country, meaning guests are served authentic fare prepared by chefs from each land. "This was a big fight within Disney," Sklar said. "Our food people wanted to operate all those restaurants in Epcot, and we said, 'No, no, no.' We have to get operators from these countries. We were after authenticity and we were not interested in contemporary. It had to be traditional."

Most of the pavilions feature attractions, shows, or films that highlight each country's endearing qualities. For those guests who wish to visit all the pavilions in one day, it's a 1.3-mile stroll along the walkway that rims the lagoon.

Epcot has evolved over the years to play into guests' willingness to take that leisurely stroll around World Showcase while enjoying the best of what each country has to offer. Popular months-long internationally themed celebrations, including Food & Wine in the fall, Flower & Garden in the spring, and the Festival of the Arts during the winter months, have added to Epcot's appeal, particularly to adults.

In addition, IllumiNations: Reflections of Earth is a nightly fireworks/laser/pyrotechnics/fire and music presentation that has been a mainstay around World Showcase Lagoon since it debuted in 1999. The show includes more than 1,100 fireworks shot from 34 different locations around the lagoon. Four barges stationed in the middle of the lagoon pump 4,000 gallons of water per minute to enhance the performance. Also floating in the lagoon during IllumiNations is a barge that shoots flames up to 60 feet in the air through 37 nozzles and a barge which supports a 28-foot-wide Earth Globe encased in 15,600 lights.

Spaceship Earth

As soon as you enter
Right in the center,
A big giant sphere
Shortly appears.

It's Spaceship Earth,
An orb of amazing worth.

Eighteen stories tall,
And a regal sight for all.

And you can walk inside,
For a spectacular ride.

A Voyage Through Yesterday and Tomorrow

There is a spaceship near the entrance of Epcot park,
That's remarkably similar to Noah's Ark.

The giant globe is anything but hollow,
Voyage through yesterday and tomorrow.

Witness future dreams and history's rebirth,
Each time you travel on Spaceship Earth.

SPACESHIP EARTH: EPCOT'S ICON TELLS THE STORY OF COMMUNICATION

When Disney's planners were designing Epcot, they were tasked with coming up with an icon, a central structure that would sum up everything the park was about while serving as a focal point for guests from both inside and outside the park. Of all the things they could have chosen, they knew a castle—used so wonderfully in the Magic Kingdoms at Disneyland and Walt Disney World— wouldn't be among the choices. A castle, with all of its dreamy, centuries-old context, just wouldn't tie in with Epcot's futuristic theming.

Disney settled on a giant geodesic dome to serve as the park's icon. Geodesic domes were first popularized by Buckminster Fuller, who also is credited with coining the phrase Spaceship Earth. Science fiction writer Ray Bradbury, who served as a consultant for Epcot during its planning stages, also contributed ideas for the attraction's storyline.

In addition to serving as Epcot's icon, the dome—which many have likened to an immense golf ball—houses a major attraction: inside Spaceship Earth is an innovative adventure that tells the history of communication, from man's first cave paintings to modern computer technology.

Spaceship Earth took 26 months to build. It is 165 feet wide and 18 stories tall and is held up by six gigantic legs, buried 160 feet into the ground. The outer layer of the ball consists of 11,324 aluminum panels, each in the shape of a triangle. Hidden behind each panel is an elaborate series of rain gutters, which funnel rainwater through the legs of the structure and out into World Showcase Lagoon— and more importantly, away from guests underneath the ball. Spaceship Earth actually consists of two layers, with the inner shell serving to support the entire structure.

Unknown to many Epcot guests is the fact that there is an underground service area, similar to the utilidors in the Magic Kingdom, located under Spaceship Earth and the nearby Innoventions, which showcases many of the latest technological advances.

Spaceship Earth takes guests in slow-moving ride vehicles from the base of the ball to the top and then back down again. The ride system is similar to, but is not, an Omnimover. The attraction's ride vehicles do travel in a continuous chain, with boarding and unloading taking place on a rotating platform, but according to former Disney designer Bob Gurr (who assisted in the development of the Omnimover system), it's not an Omnimover. "Spaceship Earth is not an Omnimover, but a one-of-a-kind vehicle conveyor totally unlike and sharing no parts with an Omnimover," Gurr said in 2012. "I disagreed so strongly with the Spaceship Earth design that I was moved to other projects—thankfully. It has had a number of redesign attempts over the years to try to reduce the high maintenance required."

Man's early attempts at communicating with one another are explored during the Spaceship Earth experience. Guests travel into the age of cavemen and wooly mammoths, then to the early Roman empire and the invention of papyrus, an early form of paper. Then, there's the creation of the alphabet, on to the printing press, radio, television, and finally, the age of computers.

Space Earth debuted with Lawrence Dobkin (some believe it was Vic Perrin, despite Marty Sklar confirming in 2008 that it was Dobkin) as its narrator, followed by newsman Walter Cronkite, actor Jeremy Irons, and finally Dame Judi Dench. The most recent version of the attraction allows guests to plot their own future and gives glimpses as to what that future might look like.

Spaceship Earth also has seen several sponsors over the years: Bell System was the original sponsor, followed by AT&T and most recently, Siemens.

Exploring The Land

The Land is a great place to go,
When it's chilly and feels like snow.

At night when you can view Orion's Belt
Or a sunny day when you think you'll melt.

No matter what the time or the weather,
No time at all could actually be any better.

The Land has numerous surprises to be unfurled,
You can shop or go Soarin' Around the World.

You can hum, or "Listen to The Land" harmonics,
As you learn about the latest uses for hydroponics.

Then take the family for a stroll through Behind the Seeds,
To see how to grow plants without pesky insects or weeds.

Stop inside Sunshine Seasons food court for a healthy bite,
Or rotate over to the Garden Grill and do dinner right.

The Land has so many more terrific surprises in store,
Beginning with Circle of Life as soon as you enter the door.

Soarin'

Soarin' high above the pale blue skies,
Looking down upon the far distant Earth.

There's quite a special insight that you'll get,
Discovering beautiful Mother's worth.

Soon the Earth below becomes an artist's palette,
Combining hues of yellow, red, and green.

They quickly blend together to become
The most beautiful quilt you've ever seen.

SOARIN' OVER AND THROUGH THE LAND

Soarin' Over California was one of the must-do attractions when Disney California Adventure swung open its gates on February 8, 2001. The virtual hang-gliding experience, which features flight motion simulator technology, was an immediate hit and spawned iterations in

Walt Disney World (which opened in 2006 as the main attraction in The Land pavilion and was known as just Soarin') and Shanghai Disneyland (which opened in 2016 as Soarin' Over the Horizon).

Imagineer Mark Sumner is credited with developing the original concept for the ride, using an Erector set and a string to create a working model. The actual ride uses a mechanical lift system, where three rows of seats at ground level are raised as high as 65 feet into the air and then out into an 80-feet wide concave, 180-degree Omnimax laser projection screen. The screen is made out of metal and mesh—metal, so that anything that falls on the screen doesn't damage it; and mesh, to allow sound to travel through it. There are 56 speakers positioned in the theater to enhance the show.

The attraction's pre-show is narrated by actor Patrick Warburton, best known for his role on the TV series *Seinfeld*. Warburton also voiced the character Kronk in *The Emperor's New Groove* and Steve Barkin in *Kim Possible*. The role of Soarin' narrator was first offered to action film star Steven Segal.

The premise of the ride is to give guests a simulated hang-gliding experience, with artificial scents and subtle breezes enhancing the feeling that you're actually soarin' through the skies. The sensation is further enhanced when the rows of seats tilt and sway in conjunction with the images projected on the screen.

The attraction fit perfectly with California Adventure's mission of celebrating the Golden State. The original version saw guests flying above several iconic California landscapes and cities, as well as along seashores and mountain cliffs. Among the sites featured in the original version of Soarin' Over California were the Golden Gate Bridge, Yosemite National Park, Napa Valley, Malibu Beach, the flight deck of the USS *Stennis*, and downtown Los Angeles. The trip culminated high above Main Street,

U.S.A., in Disneyland, where fireworks brought your flight to a rousing finish.

The adventure was enhanced immeasurably by a stirring soundtrack composed by Jerry Goldsmith.

The version now playing at Disneyland and Walt Disney World, known as Soarin' Around the World, has an updated score enhanced by Bruce Broughton. Among the familiar sites visible during the virtual flight are the Matterhorn in Switzerland, a section of the Great Wall of China, Sydney Harbor in Australia, and the Eiffel Tower. All of the sites chosen for the new show pay homage to a Disney film or character. For instance, the Great Wall of China references the Disney film *Mulan*, Sydney Harbor recalls *Finding Nemo*, and the Eiffel Tower is an homage to *Ratatouille* and Disneyland Paris.

Each attraction culminates with scenes from the park where you're experiencing it. For example, Disneyland is featured if you're riding the attraction in California Adventure, Epcot pops up on the screen if you're taking flight on Soarin' Around the World in Walt Disney World, while at Shanghai Disneyland, the city of Shanghai is featured during the finale (the new Shanghai Disneyland park hadn't opened yet during filming).

As for The Land pavilion where Soarin' is housed, it has been a fixture in the Future World section of Epcot since the park opened in 1982. On opening day, The Land featured a boat ride called Listen to the Land, a voyage through a giant greenhouse (stretching over six acres) which is still in operation today. During the boat tour, a variety of fruits and vegetables are grown hydroponically. There also are fish farms in view during the tour. All the fruits, vegetables, and fish grown in what is now known as Living with the Land are served in Epcot restaurants.

Speaking of restaurants, The Land houses two. One is called Chip 'n' Dale's Harvest Feast at the Garden Grill, which features character dining. What makes this restaurant special is the fact that the seating area rotates ever so slowly, giving guests great views from above sections of the Living with the Land attraction. Also inside The Land is Sunshine Seasons, offering a wide variety of food choices, from pastries and rotisserie chicken, to seasonal soups, salads, sandwiches, and desserts. The area was known as the Farmers Market when The Land opened.

In the space now occupied by Soarin' was an Audio-Animatronics show called Kitchen Kabaret, which featured a cast of wise-cracking fruits and vegetables in a rousing musical show with a message about good nutrition. A variety of Audio-Animatronics characters, such as Mr. Eggz and Mr. Hamm, had the guests laughing out loud with their corny jokes. The show closed in 1994 and was replaced by Food Rocks, an updated look at nutrition through the eyes of fruit and veggie rockers. Food Rocks was replaced by Soarin' in 2006.

The final attraction featured in The Land was The Circle of Life: An Environmental Fable, a film that dealt with conservation through the eyes of *The Lion King*'s Timon and Pumbaa. It closed in February of 2018.

One of the most unique aspects of The Land pavilion is the entryway, which includes 3,000 square-feet of mosaics, with 150,000 pieces of marble, stone, glass, and gold. The father and daughter-in-law team of Hanns and Monika Scharff spent three months installing the massive work of art. The two also were responsible for tile murals in Cinderella Castle in the Magic Kingdom.

Life in the Fast Lane

Buckle up and join the race,
Encircle the track at a rapid pace.

Secure belongings before you depart,
It's a ride for the young and the young at heart.

But ask your doctor and get her OK,
Before you start whizzing away.

ON THE FAST TRACK AT TEST TRACK

Test Track, sponsored by Chevrolet, is one of the most popular attractions in Epcot, in part because it appeals to those folks who yearn for a high-speed thrill ride.

During the penultimate section of the attraction, your "test vehicle" reaches speeds pushing 65 mph on the slot-car track outside the main building, which is unheard of for a theme park ride. Guests standing near the wheel-shaped pavilion are taken aback by the high-pitched, screaming sound of the cars racing overhead—not to mention seeing the track actually sway from the force of the cars thundering above.

Test Track debuted in 1999 after two years of on-again, off-again planned opening dates. The attraction, which replicates an automobile proving ground, replaced World of Motion, an original Future World attraction that debuted with the rest of the park on October 1, 1982.

World of Motion, sponsored by General Motors, told the story of transportation, starting with the early days of sailing, flying, and wheeled vehicles. The attraction culminated with a chaotic "city scene," where modes of transportation from the early years (horse-drawn vehicles) literally collided with "modern" motorized cars, buses, and trucks. The experience concluded with a viewing of a collection of GM's model cars and proto-types in the Transcenter. Surprisingly, those futuristic cars on display became the most photographed area in all of Epcot at the time.

After World of Motion closed in 1996, GM decided to up its game by presenting an experience that allowed guests to take part in putting a car through its paces on a test track. Your ride vehicle, which seated six and was designed in the shape of an actual sports car, encountered a series of tests (braking, handling, extreme heat, and cold) before pushing the limits on the high-speed test track, with sharp banks and turns before hurtling down a long straightaway.

Although the announced opening date for Test Track was May 1997, the new ride didn't open until December 1999 as a series of technical issues delayed its debut. Once it opened, however, Test Track became the must-do attraction in all of Epcot, with wait times often exceeding 90 minutes.

The General Motors version of Test Track closed in April of 2012 for refurbishment and was reopened nine months later with a new sponsor (Chevrolet) and an updated experience. Along a new, interactive queue, guests could now design their own "dream vehicle" before putting it through its paces—still culminating with that thrilling 65-mph sprint along the outdoor track. Afterwards, guests can pose for photos with their car and view Chevrolet's newest model cars.

The Test Track ride system, though problematic at the onset, has been perfected to the point where a similar system was put into use at Disney California Adventure. Radiator Springs Racers in Carsland has been thrilling guests ever since the *Cars*-themed attraction opened in 2012, pitting two cars in a side-by-side road race through Monument Valley.

Ellen's Energy Adventure

From the start of Earth,
At its moment of birth.

From normal to stranger.
To ecosystems often in danger.

Ellen made it very comical,
While Bill Nye made it educational.

If you've ever taken the ride,
You know it was great inside.

But, alas, now it's gone forever,
To make room for a new endeavor.

THE UNIVERSE OF ENERGY /
ELLEN'S ENERGY ADVENTURE

At one point in time, comedienne/television-host/ actress Ellen DeGeneres was one of the most recognizable celebrities at Walt Disney World. It started when Disney-MGM Studios opened a faux book store/real coffee shop called Buy the Book. The setting was an exact replica of the book store run by Ms. DeGeneres' character Ellen Morgan during the hit TV show *Ellen*, which aired from 1994–1998.

In 1996, DeGeneres took center stage when the re-imagined main attraction in the Universe of Energy pavilion at Epcot's Future World became known as Ellen's Energy Adventure. Around the same time, The Living Seas attraction, also in Epcot, was updated and renamed The Seas with Nemo and Friends, with one of those friends being Dory, the absent-minded blue tang fish voiced by DeGeneres in both *Finding Nemo* and *Finding Dory*.

The original Universe of Energy attraction, which opened with the rest of Epcot in 1982, featured a theater seating system that gently transported guests throughout the pavilion. A film depicting the history of fossil fuels was shown. At that point, the seemingly stationary rows of seats came apart in sections and were rolled into a part of the building where they "traveled" back to prehistoric times to view life-size dinosaur dioramas, all the while learning about the importance of energy.

One of the most appealing and environmentally friendly aspects of the Universe of Energy was the fact that the pavilion's roof was covered with two acres of photovoltaic cells, which converted Florida's strong sunlight to electricity—electricity that helped power the attraction.

The updated version, which debuted in 1996, starred DeGeneres, Bill Nye "The Science Guy," actress Jamie Lee Curtis, and game show host Alex Trebek in a humorous look at a variety of energy sources, including fossil fuels, solar and hydroelectric power, as well as the history of energy production and the quest for new energy sources. The attraction used the same moving theater system as the original and a new introductory film was introduced. The dinosaur dioramas were refreshed and some new "terrible lizards" were added to the mix, as was an Audio-Animatronics figure of DeGeneres herself.

On August 13, 2017, the Universe of Energy pavilion was closed for good. A new roller-coaster attraction, based on the Guardians of the Galaxy franchise, is currently in the works.

Mexico

Come travel with me to old Mexico,
And learn about legends from days long ago.

Aztec pyramids with carvings outside,
Specular views of the Mexican countryside.

Ancient fables with romantic words,
Tropical forests with colorful birds.

Mexico treasures are waiting for you,
Discover the old as well as the new.

The San Angel Inn

In La Hacienda de San Ángel you can
Dine under the moon-lit sky.

Enjoying your romantic evening,
As festive boats slowly glide by.

Twilight provides a tranquil refuge
From the heat of the daytime sun.

And a very delightful respite
After a full day of frolic and fun

The Mexico Pyramid

Discover adventures hidden within
An Aztec pyramid in Epcot's Mexico.

Pre-Colombian artifacts and treasures
Offer insights on several things to know.

A festive boat ride with the three caballeros
And a marketplace with authentic gifts and fare.

Mariachi musicians will play for your delight
And you may meet Donald Duck while you're there.

TAKING A TRIP SOUTH OF THE BORDER

The Mexico pavilion in Epcot opened with the rest of World Showcase on October 1, 1982. The exterior of the building resembles a Mesoamerican pyramid, typical of many structures that dot our neighbor to the south. Several times during the day, a mariachi band performs near the steps of the distinctive building.

The pavilion offers a variety of experiences that truly embody Mexican culture. After entering, guests pass through a gallery of Mexican artwork, called the Animales Fantasticos collection. After walking down a curved ramp, there's a straw market-type village setting located in the main section of the pavilion, with a variety of shops selling authentic trinkets and souvenirs, from sombreros to ceramics. There also are stores that offer more high-end jewelry and clothing.

The two main features of the Mexico pavilion are a themed restaurant and a boat ride.

The San Angel Inn restaurant offers guests authentic Mexican cuisine in what appears to be an outdoor, early evening setting. The San Angel Inn is an homage to Mexico City's most famous restaurant of the same name, which opened in 1692. The table-service venue also serves margaritas and tequilas. As guests dine, they can look out onto a placid lagoon. Beyond the waterway is a pyramid with a smoking volcano that erupts on cue every few minutes.

Adjacent to the restaurant is the entrance to the Gran Fiesta Tour Starring the Three Caballeros, an entertaining and informative "it's a small world"-type boat ride which highlights many of Mexico's natural wonders. When the Mexico pavilion opened in 1982, the attraction was called El Rio del Tiempo. The ride was updated in 2007 and became the Gran Fiesta Tour, which featured Donald, Panchito, and Jose—aka the Three Caballeros—who were featured in the 1945 movie of the same name. *The Three Caballeros* was Disney's first combined animated/ live-action feature film. It was a film that grew out of a good-will tour that Walt, Lillian, and a group of his most talented artists took to South America. Known as El Grupo, Walt and his entourage were greeted by adoring fans wherever they stopped in South America.

Outside the pavilion proper, guests can enjoy Mexican food and beverages in a less formal setting at either La Hacienda de San Angel, Le Cantina de San Angel, or La Cava del Tequila.

Norway

The enchanted land of the midnight sun,
Filled with beautiful valleys and fjords.

Ancient tales are viewed with reverence,
Yet no man's word is as sacred as the Lord's.

Wild reindeer graze on tall mountain tops,
Covered with virgin white snow.

Odin's fair maidens guard Valhalla's gates,
Where true Norse heroes hope to go.

Frozen Ever After

Cruise to Arendelle with Queen Elsa and Anna,
Sail the waters encircled with sparkling snow.

Along your Nordic voyage you can visit
With many characters you'd love to know.
Olaf the snowman will make you chuckle,
Kristoff will play with his reindeer Sven.
Loving Momma Bulda and Papa Cliff Troll
Will all encourage you to sail with them again.

Kringla Bakeri Og Kafe

Share coffee and waffles with your friends,
And enjoy a few moments of rest.

Every Norwegian knows when it comes to waffles,
Norway's are most certainly the best

NORWAY HAS COME A LONG WAY
SINCE OPENING IN 1988

The Norway pavilion is one of the most intricate and interesting exhibits in all of World Showcase. For one thing, there's grass growing on the roof of one of its buildings. To trim the grass, gardeners have to climb onto the roof and cut each blade of grass by hand.

On the ground near the grass-covered rooftop is a statue of a world-famous runner: Norwegian Olympian and former world-record marathoner, the late Grete Waitz.

Also on Norway's property is a stave church, a replica of a style of church design that was popular in Norway during the Middle Ages. The first stave church was built in 1050; there are about two dozen still in existence in Norway.

The Norway pavilion is the newest exhibition in World Showcase, having opened on October 3, 1988, six years after Epcot itself. The pavilion was a travelogue of the northern European nation, with the intent being to highlight a typical Nordic village. There is a restaurant, Akershus, which features traditional Norwegian fare, and there's also an authentic Norwegian bakery and café called Kringla Bakeri Og Kafe.

The main attraction on opening day was Maelstrom, a boat ride that highlighted Norway's mythical trolls. Throughout the journey, which at one point saw the boat (patterned after the dragon-headed craft of Eric the Red) reversing course and heading backwards, cute, if slightly menacing trolls abounded. At the end of the boat ride, guests disembarked and walked into a theater, where a film about Norway and its people was shown.

In 2013, the mega-hit movie *Frozen* was released and its success caught Disney somewhat off-guard. The company spent many months scrambling to catch up with guests' demands for Frozen-themed attractions. Since the movie was based in the fictional Norwegian town of Arendelle, it seemed logical that *Frozen* would be woven into the Norway pavilion's story. Maelstrom was closed in late 2014 and work began on making *Frozen* the main draw at Norway—and, indeed, World Showcase. In 2016, after less than two years of construction, Frozen Ever After opened as the featured attraction at Norway and has been a runaway hit ever since.

Disney's planners turned the movie theater setting into an expanded and heavily themed queue area. Although they used the same boat ride system, they remade the scenes showcased during the excursion: *Frozen* stars Elsa, Anna, Olaf, Kristof, and Sven appear prominently during the trip, while re-recorded music from the movie, featuring all of the recognizable voices from the soundtrack, can be heard. When guests are finished with the boat tour, they walk through two quaint gift shops, named Puffin's Roost and the Wandering Reindeer.

Also added to the new Norway experience is a meet-and-greet area where guests can pose for photos with Elsa and Anna. To make room for the authentic Norwegian summer cottage and mountain setting used for the photo ops, the replica of a Viking ship, which had been featured since opening day, was removed.

The Voices of Liberty

Voices as beautiful as a melodic songbird,
And proud Americans react to every word.
Patriotism abounds and love for country excels,
In a land of patriots who rang the Liberty Bell.

THE RED, WHITE, AND BLUE AMERICAN ADVENTURE

The centerpiece of World Showcase—and, indeed, the unquestioned host of the global exhibitions at Epcot—is the American Adventure, located between Italy and Japan. Guests visiting Epcot from foreign lands will learn about America's proud, yet sometimes troubled history through a stirring theatrical presentation, a 30-minute show that employs film, music, and some of the most sophisticated Audio-Animatronics figures ever presented by Disney.

The adventure begins in the rotunda of the 1800s-styled pavilion, where the *a capella* singing group the Voices of Liberty sets the mood with stirring renditions of American folk music and patriotic songs. From the rotunda, guests are led upstairs to a massive theater, where the story of America unfolds.

Combining large-screen projections as a backdrop, we learn of how America was discovered, how it grew and developed, and how and why it fought to attain its independence from Great Britain. Moreover, the show touches on the human rights struggles of Americans. Audio-Animatronics figures play a key role here: Frederick Douglas speaks out against slavery, Chief Joseph demands an end to his fellow Native Americans' suffering, and feminist Susan B. Anthony opines on the topic of equal rights for women.

Perhaps the most moving moments of the presentation come when the song "Two Brothers" is played during the segment dealing with the American Civil War. Using archival photos of the war taken by Matthew Brady, only one of the brothers—"One wore blue and one wore gray"—returns from the bloody conflict that tore our nation apart. The entire score for the presentation was recorded by the Philadelphia Orchestra.

The American Adventure's stage measures 130 feet by 50 feet, while the projection screen—the largest rear projection screen ever—is 28 feet tall and 155 feet wide. As America's story unfolds, scenes from different eras are lifted into view by a scene changer that weighs 175 tons. The operation is controlled by more than 24 computers. The film sequences used during the earlier sections of the presentation employ Disney's tried-and-true multiplane camera technique, which give the illustrations more realism.

In all, more than 35 Audio-Animatronics figures— including one of Ben Franklin, who appears to be walking up a flight of stairs at the beginning of the show—make for a stirring presentation. During the show, author Thomas Wolfe is quoted: "To every one, a chance. To all people, regardless of their birth, the right to live, to work, to better themselves, to become whatever their visions can combine to make them. This is the promise of America."

In original concepts for World Showcase, the American Adventure pavilion was to be placed at the entrance of World Showcase, between Mexico and Canada. After careful consideration, the site was moved to its present location across the lagoon.

The exterior of the American Adventure is a replica of a Colonial American manor and reflects English Georgian architecture of that time period. It is actually five stories tall, but since there were no buildings taller than two stories during the 1800s and Disney didn't want the America building to be too prominent when compared to other structures in World Showcase, the Imagineers made the building appear to be just two stories in height. John Hench was primarily responsible for selecting a color palette of red brick, white-and-green trim, and a blue-gray slate roof, inspired by the Colonial buildings of 1700s Philadelphia.

The American Adventure also includes two on-site dining options, the Liberty Inn (featuring hot dogs, Angus burgers, chicken, and salads) and the Fife and Drum Tavern (turkey legs, frozen beverages, and beer).

In addition, across the promenade from the American Adventure pavilion is the America Gardens Theatre, the premiere outdoor theater venue in World Showcase. The theater, on the shores of the World Showcase Lagoon, hosts a variety of concert series during the year in conjunction with the seasonal festivals (Flower & Garden, Festival of the Arts, and Food & Wine) hosted at Epcot. The America Gardens Theatre also hosts a stirring candlelight processional each holiday season, where a 50-piece orchestra and a choir of 400 accompany celebrity narrators in a moving retelling of the story of Christmas.

China

Knowledge passed down from generation to generation,
Wisdom taught through poetry since the first days of creation.
Intricate wood carvings that are difficult to do,
Jade of every size and texture, ceramics of white and blue.
Artisans of acrobatics, masters of defense,
China, a country that is intriguing and immense.
When you visit the China pavilion,
There are a few friendly words to say.
Hello in Chinese is pronounced Nee haoww,
How are you? is pronounced Nee haoww mah?
If you want to say 100, it is pronounced Ee-bye,
When you leave, the correct phrase is bye-bye.

WORLD SHOWCASE VISITORS
CAN FIND SERENITY IN CHINA

Guests who visit the China pavilion in World Showcase are always touched by how serene and peaceful it is.

First, visitors walk through the Zhao Yung Men, or Gate of the Golden Sun.

The ornate Hall of Prayer for Good Harvest is the focal point of the pavilion grounds, with its exquisitely detailed, three-tiered roofs hovering above elaborate walkways and ponds, where floating lotus flowers, delicate rockwork and intricate bridges set a tranquil setting.

The Hall of Prayer is a half-scale replica of the original imperial temple located just outside the Chinese capital city of Beijing. The sacred site was built in the 1400s. Inside the Epcot version of the temple, guests can enjoy an acoustically perfect experience, meaning that if they say something while standing in the middle of the temple, guests can hear their voices as they echo off the circular wall.

China is home to a CircleVision 360 film called *Reflections of China*, which debuted in 2003. The film presents a stunning overview of China, the world's most populous nation, including views of its people, culture, history, and iconic structures. When the pavilion opened in 1981, the original presentation was titled *Wonders of China: Land of Beauty, Land of Time*. In 2017, plans were set in motion to update *Reflections of China* by using next-generation digital cameras that will provide a seamless CircleVision presentation.

Guests exiting the *Reflections of China* theater may notice how tight the exit corridor is. That was done intentionally by designers in order to replicate the crowded conditions along many of the streets in China's big cities.

As with all the other World Showcase pavilions, China offers a wide variety of culinary delights. There's the Nine Dragons Restaurant, featuring fine Chinese cuisine, wine, and beer; the Lotus Blossom Café, offering egg rolls, orange chicken, and rice bowls; and Joy of Tea, with assorted teas, beverages, ice cream, and snacks.

Entertainment options in China include the Dragon Legends Acrobats, with students from Pu Yang Academy of Acrobats in China in a display of agility, strength, and balance; Si Xian, a Shanghai region folk music presentation; and the Chinese Lion Dancers, who perform during the Christmas season. China also features an expansive shopping experience, the Yong Feng Shangdian Department Store, which sells authentic Chinese furniture, kitchenware, rugs, clothing, slippers, silk, paper fans, and jewelry.

With the opening of Shanghai Disneyland in 2016, the China pavilion was updated to provide an intimate look into the newest Disney theme park experience. The Shanghai Disneyland display is located in the House of Whispering Willows Gallery.

Germany

Germany is the best location for you,
For a warm pretzel and a beer or two.
Bratwurst and strudel or a large buffet,
Germany's the place to dine any time of day.

GERMANY: FROM BEER AND BRATWURST TO HUMMELS AND OKTOBERFEST

When Germany opened as part of World Showcase in 1981, it was an exhibit that represented half a nation. In 1981, Germany was divided into two countries, East Germany and West Germany, a result of the division which occurred following the end of World War II. West Germany was a free and democratic nation, while East Germany fell under Communist rule. The city of Berlin also was divided into east and west segments, separated by the infamous Berlin Wall.

Although the Germany pavilion captured the essence of German culture and tradition, with beer, bratwurst, and Oktoberfest as a focus, it wouldn't be until 1990, when East Germany and West Germany reunified into one nation, that the true spirit of all of the people of Germany would be captured in the Epcot showplace.

As with every other pavilion in World Showcase, Germany was designed to showcase an iconic image rather than displaying a broad range of elements representing the entire country.

Guests enter Germany and walk into a cobblestoned *platz*, or plaza. The area is representative of a Bavarian village. Prominent in the *platz* is a statue of St. George slaying a dragon. St. George, the patron saint of soldiers, is said to have killed a dragon that was in the process of mauling a king's daughter, using his magical sword to accomplish the feat. To this day, most German villages have a statue of St. George displayed prominently in their courtyards as a symbol of protection.

Germany is rife with architectural elements that need a sharp eye to spot. For instance, there are two charming Hummel-styled figurines atop one of the buildings who help chime a giant glockenspiel. And Gild Hall is enhanced by elaborate figures of Philip I, Charles V, and Ferdinand I, perched on the side of the building, which was designed to replicate a merchants' hall.

On a hot and humid summer day, Germany is perhaps the best spot along the World Showcase promenade to grab a cold beer or a pretzel. Indeed, food is a main attraction in Germany, with the always popular and raucous Biergarten topping the list of culinary offerings. The Biergarten features an Oktoberfest buffet along with lively entertainment. Among the menu items are traditional schnitzel, sausage, spätzle, and or course, strudel for dessert.

Sommerfest offers guests bratwurst, German potato salad, beer, and a variety of desserts. For those with an insatiable craving for sweets, Germany also features Karamell-Kuche, which offers a variety of Werther's Original Caramel products. The nearby gift shop displays a wide range of products indicative of Germany, from soccer jerseys to Hummel figurines.

And when it comes to authentic entertainment, Margret Almer and the Bavarian Band can oompah with the best of them.

Italian Dining

Italy has a lot to see, but I recommend
Delicious brick-oven pizza with cheese.
Via Napoli Ristorante e Pizzeria
Is a family favorite that's sure to please.
There are splendid wood-fired ovens
Named after three famous volcanoes in Italy.
They're all worth waiting in line to see:
Mount Etna, Mount Vesuvius, and Stromboli.

THIS PAVILION OFFERS A SLICE OF ITALY...AND ITALIAN CUISINE

Italy is a land of world-famous and recognizable icons, from the Leaning Tower of Pisa to St. Peter's Square in Rome. When it came time to select an immediately familiar centerpiece for the Italy pavilion in World Showcase, Disney's designers chose to replicate the bell tower that is so prominent in St. Mark's Square in Venice. The Epcot tower, which stands 83 feet tall (one-fifth the size of the original), is exquisite in every detail, right down to the gold leaf-covered angel which resides atop the structure.

The bell tower serves to draw guests into the pavilion's entry plaza, or piazza, highlighted by a replica of the Doge's Palace, built between the 9th and 16th centuries and which represents both Gothic and Renaissance architectural styles. There also are two columns that adorn the entrance of the piazza: one features the statue of a lion, which is believed to be guarding Venice, while the other depicts St. Theodore slaying a dragon. Further along in the piazza is the Fontana di Nettuno, an homage to the Italian sculptor Gian Lorenzo Bernini. On the opposite side of the entry piazza, across from the promenade, is the Isola del Lago, which abuts the World Showcase Lagoon and is intended to embrace Venice's aquatic heritage. The lagoon's waters wash up to mooring posts and gondolas, reflecting Venice's signature canals and waterways.

But perhaps the most iconic element of Italy is its food, represented quite tastefully by two restaurants and a wine cellar.

Via Napoli Ristorante e Pizzeria is the crown jewel of the Italy pavilion. Via Napoli is best-known for its wood-fired pizzas. Guests can watch as the pizzas are being prepared and then placed into the restaurant's massive brick ovens. Also on the menu at Via Napoli are Italian pastas and piatti alla parmigiana, all topped off with tiramisu for desert.

Tutto Italia Ristorante offers guests a less formal, though no less tasty offering of Italian dishes, while Tutto Gusto Wine Cellar specializes in fine Italian wines and imported cheeses.

The Japan Pavilion

Buy a string of pearls
Or a sparkling ring.
In the Japan pavilion,
You can buy most anything.
Embroidered kimonos,
Or a miniature tree.
Embellished chopsticks,
Or authentic Japanese tea.

Japan

Like an empress adorned with pearls,
You proudly display a regal crown of snow.
Carefully watching over the land,
And the people you treasure so.
Your deep blue lakes reflect the sun,
Like sapphires bathed in a morning dew.
While you humbly give reverence
To the heavens high above you.

DRUMMING UP INTEREST IN THE
LAND OF THE RISING SUN

Epcot has always been considered a visual masterpiece, blending a wide variety of architectural styles to embrace many of the world's cultures.

But when it comes to the Japan pavilion, guests are enveloped by both its visual and auditory cues. From just about every section of Epcot's World Showcase, guests can hear the unmistakable sounds of taiko, the Japanese style of drumming that is performed five times a day near the entrance of the pavilion by a group called Matsuriza. The energetic musicians pound on drums that range in size from 6 inches to 6 feet tall. It is both a musical treat and visual delight for guests.

Taiko serves as a window into the rest of the Japan experience, which has been described by many as both serene and dramatic. Disney's creative staff took into account many traditional Japanese design elements, like balance, harmony, simplicity, formality, and delicacy.

In the lagoon near the entrance to Japan is a traditional torii gate. This type of gate can be found throughout Japan. They are believed to elicit good fortune and purification.

The torii gate is just one of several meticulously crafted re-creations of actual Japanese structures.

A prominent pagoda dominates the landscape in Japan. It is modeled after the Horyugi Temple, which was built in the 8th century. It contains five stories, with each representing the tenets of the Buddhist universe: earth, water, fire, wind, and heaven. The Yakitori Tea House was inspired by the Katsura Imperial Villa.

The food choices in Japan are representative of the country's diverse tastes.

Teppen Edo, the Japan pavilion's signature restaurant, features steak, seafood and chicken, all grilled in front of you by master Teppan chefs who put on a show as you watch. Tokyo Dining offers sushi, bento boxes, grilled items, as well as traditional Japanese cuisine.

Katsura Grill has teriyaki combinations, udon noodles, sushi, and curry, while Kabuki Café offers shaved ice, sushi snacks, Japanese beer, and other traditional beverages.

The Japan pavilion also takes pride in its museum-quality displays, which showcase products that were proudly made in Japan. For example, the Tin Toy Exhibit in Japan is among the most popular collections in all of World Showcase. In addition, guests can take a leisurely stroll through a gift shop filled with traditional Japanese wares.

Morocco

Beautiful brightly colored ceramics,
The aroma of North African cuisine.

Henna decorations for a new bride,
And handcrafted ceramic tajne.

Morocco is as diverse as any country
That you have probably ever seen.

EXOTIC MOROCCO JOINED THE EPCOT FOLD IN 1984

When cruise ships pass through the Strait of Gibraltar—as the *Disney Magic* does each year after spending the summer plying the waters of the Mediterranean Sea—most passengers make it a point to view the majestic Rock of Gibraltar to the right, one of the most photographed natural wonders in Europe. On the other side of the ship, all but forgotten, is Africa. More specifically, the exotic country of Morocco, with its imposing mountainous terrain.

Morocco became a member of the World Showcase family on September 7, 1984, some two years after Epcot opened. The pavilion is modeled after the Moroccan cities of Casablanca, Fes, and Marrakesh. It features courtyards and winding corridors that connect guests to shops and eateries in a lively bazaar setting. The most distinctive structure in Morocco is its minaret, a lighthouse-type structure that towers above the pavilion.

The Gallery of Arts and History in the pavilion lets guests learn about the lifestyle and culture of the Moroccan people, while the Fes House offers a glimpse into how a typical Moroccan family lives. Sprinkled throughout the exterior of the pavilion are plants native to North Africa, including citrus trees, date palms, and olive trees.

Unlike World Showcase's other pavilions, Morocco proudly flies its nation's flag. That's because the Moroccan pavilion is sponsored by the country's king, and not by corporations.

"There's an organization called the Bureau of International Expositions (BIE) and their rules are that no country tied to their organization can be in a permanent world's fair, if you will, or expo, for more than a year," former Imagineering executive Marty Sklar said. That rule "virtually eliminated countries from participating. If you notice, you don't see any flags flying in front of countries in the World Showcase. There's no nation representation."

Except for Morocco. "When the king speaks, that changes everything—so Morocco is there as a country," Sklar said. "The king decided he wanted to be in, but he's probably not a member of the BIE."

The king also had a hand in the design of the pavilion, sending his royal craftsman to supervise the creation of the mosaics, tiles, carvings, paintings, and other work.

Morocco features three dining options: Restaurant Marrakesh, which offers beef, lamb, and chicken dinners with a lively belly dancing show thrown in to spice things up; the Tangierine Café (chicken and lamb shawama, wraps, and salads), and Spice Road Table, featuring Mediterranean specialty entrees, small plates, wine, beer, and organic sangria.

France

The lunch place I choose to be,
Is Les Halles Boulangerie Patisserie.

With an aroma of pastry as fine as can be,
What better place is there for me?

For a tasty croissant and a burgundy,
Or a lobster bisque, fresh from the sea.

The Eiffel Tower

Iron woven into a beautiful lace nest,
Creating the finest perch that could ever be.

Places frozen in history captured below,
City Lights sparkle like a Christmas tree.

Every time I return to Epcot's France,
The tower becomes more beautiful to me.

CAPTURING THE BEAUTY AND ROMANCE OF PARIS AND THE FRENCH COUNTRYSIDE

When guests cross over the bridge that separates the World Showcase Lagoon and the International Gateway entrance to Epcot, they see a stunning replica of the Eiffel Tower in the distance. That's the calling card for France, a pavilion that captures the history and romance of Paris, as well as the stately beauty of the French countryside.

At the base of the bridge, to the right, guests are greeted by a lush garden reminiscent of the displays at the majestic Palace of Versailles. Nearby, at the water's edge, there are small boats, bicycles, and other accoutrements that visitors to Paris will see as they stroll along the banks of the Seine River. To the left, guests are greeted by Chefs de France, an authentic French brasserie reminiscent of the scores of restaurants that permeate the byways of Paris.

The main attraction in France is a film, *Impressions de France*, which gives guests a panoramic tour of the French countryside in all of its grandeur and charm. You'll see stately castles, colorful hot-air balloon races, and flyovers of majestic, snow-covered mountain peaks. There also are more intimate glimpses of Paris, the City of Lights, from Notre Dame Cathedral to the Louvre to the Grand Palais to the Champs-Elysees to a river cruise along the Seine.

Prominent among these Parisian snapshots is the seemingly ever-present Eiffel Tower. Epcot's version of the lattice spire is one-tenth the size of the original. When Disney's Imagineers went about the task of replicating the Parisian icon, they consulted Gustave Eiffel's original blueprints. They even went the extra step to give Epcot's Eiffel Tower a brownish hue, which was the color of the tower when it debuted in 1889 as the entrance portal to the Paris World's Fair.

As you might expect, the France pavilion is brimming with food options. In addition to the aforementioned Chefs de France, there's Monsieur Paul, which offers fine French dining, Les Halles Boulangerie-Patisserie (artisan breads, sandwiches, pastries, and baked goods), and L'Artisan des Glaces (house-made ice cream and sorbets).

Disney fans who visit Paris will no doubt make their way to Disneyland Paris, just 20 miles to the west of the city in the town of Marne-la-Vallee. The park is divided into two sections: Disneyland Park and Walt Disney Studios. One of the most talked-about attractions in Walt Disney Studios is Ratatouille: L'Adventure Totalement Toquee de Remy.

In the attraction, guests are "shrunk" to the size of a rat as they enter the world embraced in the hit Disney film *Ratatouille*. Guests duck, dive, and dodge their way through dozens of obstacles in Gusteau's kitchen in a thrilling adventure. In 2017, plans were finalized to bring the attraction to Epcot, where it will enjoy a permanent home in France. Ratatouille: The Adventure is expected to open in 2021.

The United Kingdom Pavilion

Stop in England for a glass of ale or a cup of tea,
Visit the Crown & Crest for some rose-scented potpourri.

In Scotland, you can buy a tie in the plaid of your clan,
The Sportsman Shoppe has a soccer ball for every sports fan.

At the Magic of Wales, you'll find beautiful jewelry,
The Tea Caddy has some delicious biscuits and Irish tea.

Queen's Table has Belleek china decorated with shamrocks,
The Toy Soldier has games and costumes toys for little tots.

When you are finished, walk over to the Rose and Crown,
With the wind right, see the fireworks from the best place in town.

JOLLY OL' ENGLAND
COMES TO LIFE AT EPCOT

Care for a spot of tea? How about some fish and chips? After you've enjoyed a cold pint at the Rose and Crown, why not stroll over to an authentic English garden and listen to a rock band performing some of the most memorable songs by the Beatles or other stars of the British Invasion? These are some of the experiences that will delight your senses during a visit to the United Kingdom.

The UK pavilion, located near the International Gateway entrance of World Showcase, is an authentic re-creation of some of England's most characteristic architectural styles, from thatched-roofed countryside cottages to a stately city square to two castle replicas. Indeed, eight different styles are represented in the United Kingdom's space: Victorian, London, Yorkshire, Manor, Tudor, Georgian, Hyde Park, Regency, and Shakespearean.

The United Kingdom pavilion opened on October 1, 1982. For the first month of operation, formal ceremonies, including a presentation of the Union Jack flag, were held there.

There are three dining options available: the Rose and Crown Pub features pub fare, with British ales, lagers, and stouts on tap, as well as snacks.

The Rose and Crown Dining Room is a more formal setting, with UK favorites such as steak, shepherd's pie, and corned beef. The motto of the restaurant, as seen on the menus and at the entrance, is "Otium cum Dignitate," which is Latin for "Leisure and Dignity."

Lastly, the Yorkshire Country Fish House offers traditional fish and chips, beverages, and beer.

Canada

As soon as you enter Hotel du Canada,
You will feel welcome and right at home.
Canada is a land of awesome beauty,
That is located very near to our own.
The Victoria Gardens are lovely,
Regardless of the time of year.
And the kiosks are great places,
To purchase cold weather gear.
Fine cuisine is available
At the restaurant Le Cellier.
Their French onion soup,
Is a superlative best-seller.
However you decide to
Begin your Canadian adventure,

End your tour with some Canadian brew;
It's a delicious thirst quencher

O CANADA! THERE'S A BROAD MIX
OF NORTHERN EXPERIENCES

Diverse Canada is comprised of ten provinces and three territories. To capture its diversity, Disney's planners were tasked with designing everything from mountain peaks to lush gardens to a stately hotel, all representative of our neighbor to the north.

The grounds of the Canada pavilion are stunning. First, there's the beautiful Victoria Gardens, which were inspired by the Butchart Gardens, near Victoria, British Columbia. In the Victoria Gardens, there are winding walkways, colorful plantings, and small ponds and streams—the perfect setting to relax and enjoy a quiet moment amid the hustle-and-bustle of World Showcase. Epcot's horticultural team took the added step of acclimating the plants used in the garden to Florida's often oppressive weather, a process that lasted two years.

"Towering" over Victoria Gardens is Epcot's version of the Canadian Rocky Mountains. Disney's designers used forced perspective to make these mountain peaks seem a lot larger than they are in real life. The rugged mountain range and its surrounding foliage hints at Canada's beautiful, though still-untamed wilderness.

Next, there's the stunning Hotel du Canada, a limestone building inspired by the Chateau Laurier in Ottawa. The Hotel du Canada is meant to symbolize Canadians' pioneering drive westward. Near the hotel is the Northwest Mercantile and Trading Post, another nod toward the march west. Included in this area are several distinctive, hand-carved totem poles.

Finally, a smaller village, recalling Prince Edward Island, Nova Scotia, and New Brunswick, celebrates the Canadian maritime provinces

The featured show in Canada, nestled in a log cab-in-type setting, is the 360-degree CircleVision film *O Canada!*, a stunningly beautiful, richly detailed travelogue that serves up a panoramic view of all the nation has to offer. On their way to the theater, however, guests get to experience what it's like to walk through a lush mountain grotto, complete with a crashing waterfall and a stone stairway. It's the perfect table-setter for the film that's just a few steps ahead.

Also featured in Canada is Le Cellier Steakhouse, where steaks, pasta, seafood, and of course, Canadian beer tops the menu. Canadian-themed entertainment rounds out the diverse offerings featured in this magnificent pavilion.

Lighting the Night
Around World Showcase

Even on a warm night you can feel the heat of the fire
Grow more intense as it grows higher and higher.

Like a strong gust of wind blowing out a candle,
You have more excitement than you can handle.

Your heart begins to beat stronger and faster,
As those around you change from gasp to laughter.

A history lesson with fireworks and a musical arrangement,
All disguised as a marvelous evening's entertainment.

Glistening waters all aglow with magical sparkling lights,
Makes today one of your most favorite vacation nights.

ILLUMINATIONS: REFLECTIONS OF EARTH

Night-time shows featuring fireworks and music have been a Walt Disney World staple since the Electrical Water Pageant debuted in the waters of Seven Seas Lagoon in 1972. That show spawned a variety of iterations, including the Main Street Electrical Parade, and themed fireworks shows, all enhanced by stirring musical scores, over every Disney park, save for Animal Kingdom.

At Epcot, shows over the World Showcase Lagoon—
and not just under the cover of darkness—have been
a long-standing tradition.

Epcot's first stab at night-time entertainment came
right after the park opened in 1982. It was called Carnival
de Lumière, featured fountain and fireworks barges, and
could only be viewed from between the Mexico and Canada
pavilions. That show was followed the next summer by A
New World Fantasy, a more ambitious display.

As computer sophistication became more advanced,
so, too, did Disney's desire to ramp up its night-time
shows at Epcot.

In 1984, Epcot debuted Laserphonic Fantasy,
a quantum leap forward from the existing A New World
Fantasy show. Laserphonic Fantasy placed fountain and
fireworks barges around a central barge, which contained
lighting and fog effects. The barge also had the ability to
emit laser projections. Laser projection booths also were
installed and triangulated at the Canada, Mexico, and
American Adventure pavilions. The sweeping nature of
Laserphonic Fantasy allowed guests to view the show
from just about any location around World Showcase.

As part of Walt Disney World's 15th anniversary cel-
ebration in 1986, Epcot was home to an afternoon show
over the World Showcase Lagoon called Skyleidoscope.
The show was themed as a clash of good vs evil and fea-
tured a variety of water and airborne components. There
were acrobatic aircraft, ultra-lights, and delta-winged
kites above, with high-speed boats, hovercraft, and sail
boats below, all engaged in a colorful, high-speed chore-
ography over and above the lagoon's waters.

In 1988, Epcot debuted IllumiNations, the brainchild
of Walt Disney Creative Entertainment in collaboration
with Walt Disney Imagineering. IllumiNations took
Laserphonic Fantasy to the next level, expanding the show
to include all of the nations' building façades surrounding

World Showcase as a canvas of color. A variety of effects—
including fireworks shot from barges and from along the
lagoon's edges, laser beams, strobe lights, theater lights,
and enhanced use of floating barges with water projec-
tions—combined to broaden the scope of the presentation.
A stirring new soundtrack helped to elevate the show into
one of the most must-see attractions in all of WDW.

In conjunction with the millennial celebration in
2000, IllumiNations was further enhanced and became
known as IllumiNations 2000: Reflections of Earth.
More sophisticated technology was added to the mix,
as was an "Earth Globe" barge, which helped to tell the
story of our planet. The Earth Globe is 28 feet in diam-
eter and sits atop a 10-foot pedestal. It features the
world's first spherical video display system (the globe is
wrapped in 15,600 LED clusters). The Earth Globe, which
has a driver on board, begins the show on the edge of
the World Showcase Lagoon before it gradually journeys
out to the center of the waterway to be seen from any
vantage point around the lagoon.

The show was supposed to be shut down following
the millennium, but it proved to be so popular that it
remains a night-time fixture at Epcot. IllumiNations
has been tweaked over the years to include a Christmas
holiday version.

CHAPTER THREE

Disney's Hollywood Studios

The Studios

The Great Movie Ride is gone,
Hollywood's Chinese theater is, too.

But I understand that Mickey Mouse
Has wonderful attractions in store for you.

Because Disney always thinks twice
Before anything they choose to do,

I heard Mickey and Minnie's Railroad
May add a station at the Studios for you.

Photo Pass

See Jedi Knights from throughout the galaxy,
A princess from a magical Nordic fantasy.

Enjoy some fresh Anaheim Produce coolers,
While listening to new Star Wars Land rumors.

Use your PhotoPass to take a photo with all,
So you can hang all those pictures on your wall.

The ABC Commissary

The lasagna is plentiful and supreme,
And the burgers are an absolute dream.

When you want to eat in the ABC Commissary,
You can call ahead whenever you're in a hurry.

CHANGE HAS BEEN THE NAME OF THE
GAME AT DISNEY'S HOLLYWOOD STUDIOS

Of all the theme parks in Walt Disney World, Disney's Hollywood Studios has seen the most change since opening in 1989 at a cost of $500 million.

To begin with, the park actually grew out of Disney's desire to create an entertainment-themed *attraction* for the Future World section of Epcot. The proposed attraction was to touch on three key elements of entertainment: movies, television, and radio. The initial concept was to take guests through the great moments from movies, then a television sound stage, and finally, a display of how important sound is to the movie industry. But the idea of a single attraction quickly outgrew those plans and it blossomed into an entire theme park.

That park was known as the Disney-MGM Studios when it opened, tying it to the bygone era of classic Hollywood films of the 1930s and 1940s. The premise of "the Studios" was to make park guests feel as if they had walked right into the middle of a film set, either a movie or a television show. Soundstages and backlot sets combined with themed attractions to give guests a taste of all the glitz and glamour of the Hollywood that never was, but always will be. And, to add to the realism, scenes from actual movies and TV shows were filmed there.

The entrance to the park was inspired by the Streamline Moderne style of architecture displayed at the legendary Pan-Pacific Auditorium in Hollywood, designed by the firm owned by Walt Disney's good friend, Welton Becket. The main thoroughfare of the Studios is Hollywood Boulevard, which isn't modeled after any particular street in Los Angeles, but looks typical of just about any street in LaLa Land, complete with palm trees and trendy-looking store fronts. It's the Studios' version of Main Street, U.S.A.

Looming up ahead was the park's signature attraction, housed inside a stunning replica of Grauman's Chinese

Theater, complete with the handprints of many famous stars imprinted on the walkways near the entrance. The Great Movie Ride took guests on a tour of movie history, with the aid of 59 stunningly realistic Audio-Animatronics figures and several live actors. Scenes from classic movies like *Footlight Parade, Singin' in the Rain, Raiders of the Lost Ark, Tarzan,* and *Casablanca* were replicated during the attraction. The penultimate scene was a trip through *The Wizard of Oz,* the beginning of the Yellow Brick Road, and an appearance by the Wicked Witch. The ride concluded with a film montage of some of moviedom's greatest hits.

At the original Grauman's, which opened in 1927 and hosted a myriad of events, including the Academy Awards, Walt Disney premiered some of his most important films, like *Mary Poppins* and *The Jungle Book.*

(The Great Movie Ride closed for good in 2017, with an attraction called Mickey & Minnie's Runaway Railway currently in the works to replace it.)

The other attractions in the park put a premium on audience participation. They included the Monster Sound Show, featuring Chevy Chase and Martin Short; Superstar Television, where guests got the chance to "co-star" on several classic TV episodes; the Honey, I Shrunk the Kids movie set adventure; and the Backstage Studio Tour, featuring Catastrophe Canyon.

Additions to the park a few years after opening included the Indiana Jones Epic Stunt Spectacular!, Jim Henson's Muppet*Vision 3-D, and the Voyage of the Little Mermaid. In addition, the park featured dining options themed to the movies, such as Hollywood Brown Derby, Mama Melrose's, Sci-Fi Dine-In Theater Restaurant, and the ABC Commissary. Over the years, additional attractions, including Twilight Zone Tower of Terror, Beauty and the Beast: Live on Stage, Star Tours, Rock 'n' Roller Coaster Starring Aerosmith, and Toy Story Mania!, have enhanced the Hollywood Studios experience exponentially.

The park is currently undergoing a massive overhaul, with the additions of entire new lands devoted to the Star Wars franchise and another featuring attractions themed to the Toy Story movies expected to add luster to a park already devoted to glitz and glamour.

The new Star Wars Land, to be called Star Wars: Galaxy's Edge, will open in both Disneyland and Disney's Hollywood Studios some time in 2019. Both will encompass 14 acres. Galaxy's Edge will be a totally immersive Star Wars experience on "the remote frontier outpost on the planet Batuu," with attractions, shows, and restaurants. In Florida, a Star Wars-themed luxury hotel is planned adjacent to the new land.

The recently opened Toy Story Land is 11 acres and incorporates the existing Toy Story Mania! The featured attraction in the new land is a family-friendly roller coaster called Slinky Dog Dash.

Rock 'n' Roll on a Roller Coaster

When it comes to rides, I'm rather picky,
Especially when they speed by so quickly.
But there's one coaster that I totally love,
It fits my personality like a tailored glove.
Music flows through my ears and my hair,
No matter how often I ride, I love it there.

A LOOPY ATTRACTION THAT
KEEPS YOU IN THE DARK

Every theme park attraction created by the folks at Walt Disney Imagineering has a common thread, whether it's a placid ride geared to young children or a heart-pounding roller coaster: it must be based on a great story.

In the case of Rock 'n' Roller Coaster Starring Aerosmith, that story centers around the rock band Aerosmith as they climb into a stretch limo and race from a recording session, through the streets of Los Angeles, to a concert venue. You, as their invited guest, go along for the ride of your life.

The mood is set outside the attraction. As guests walk from Sunset Boulevard and make a left to the entrance of the venue, they are greeted by a 40-foot tall guitar with a 32-foot-long neck that cleverly segues into a roller-coaster track. After entering the main building, guests walk along the queue, which features a variety of rock music-themed posters and vintage album covers on display. The queue winds its way into an observation area, where guests watch as the members of Aerosmith wrap up their recording session at G-Force Records. Suddenly, they realize that if they don't hurry, they'll be late for their concert on the other side of Los Angeles.

As their invited guest, you get to ride with them in their stretch "limousine," which looks like a car, but is actually three connected coaster vehicles that seat a total of 12 riders. Once all the passengers board the car and secure their individual shoulder harnesses, the car gently rolls out to a main "street," where a red light brings your car to a halt. A short countdown ensues before the light goes from red to green and the car blasts off into the darkness.

Rock 'n' Roller Coaster was the first Disney attraction to feature a linear induction motor launch, a technique that uses electromagnets which engage in rapid-fire sequence to propel the vehicle from 0 to 60 mph in just 2.8 seconds. During the race to the concert, guests experience two rollover loops and one corkscrew turn along the 3,403-foot-long track. As your car careens through the streets of LA, the music of Aerosmith is blasted through loudspeakers; indeed, there are a total of 125 speakers positioned inside each limo. There are three different soundtracks, depending on the limo you board.

The ride takes place in complete darkness, although lighted road signs are visible at times during the trip.

Riders experience a force of nearly 5Gs, which is more than the force astronauts were subjected to during the launch of the space shuttle (3Gs).

Rock 'n' Roller Coaster Starring Aerosmith debuted in 1998, about four years after the nearby Twilight Zone Tower of Terror. In designing Rock 'n' Roller Coaster, Disney's Imagineers made it a point to build the main section of the attraction as far away from the tower as possible, so as not to compete with the latter's imposing structure.

A VIP Dessert

To secure some fabulous seats,
And some quite tasty treats,

VIP Service will cost you more,
But you're assured magic galore.

If you're on a seldom-taken vacation,
Or celebrate a very special occasion.

Request VIP Dessert for Fantasmic!
I think this package is fantastic.

Great seats, a stage show, and fireworks,
I think it's the best show in the universe.

FANTASMIC! LIGHTS THE NIGHT AT HOLLYWOOD STUDIOS

Disney's creative staff often refers to the last show of the night in its parks as "a kiss goodnight." It's their way of saying "thanks for coming, see ya real soon."

Fantasmic! is the grand finale—the "kiss goodnight— at Disneyland, Hollywood Studios, and Tokyo DisneySea. All three shows feature fireworks, a boatload of Disney characters, live actors, pyrotechnics, lasers, water screen projections, and classic Disney songs.

The original Fantasmic! debuted at Disneyland in 1992. Walt Disney Creative Entertainment, in collaboration with Walt Disney Feature Animation and Walt Disney

Imagineering, came up with a night-time spectacular using Tom Sawyer Island and the Rivers of America as their stage set. The area around New Orleans Square was expanded and reworked to include terraced walkways to accommodate the influx of guests for the show.

Tom Sawyer Island was modified to be able to support the live-action segments of the show, while the Rivers of America's main tenants—the Sailing Ship *Columbia* and the *Mark Twain* Riverboat—were pressed into duty to serve as floating stages for different segments of the presentation.

The storyline of Fantasmic! at both Disneyland and Hollywood Studios takes guests into Mickey Mouse's vivid imagination, a journey that culminates in a battle against a host of some of Disney's most notorious villains, including a towering Maleficent dragon, which measures 50 feet tall and has a 50-foot-wide wingspan. It's a classic good vs. evil story—with Mickey, as you might expect, emerging victorious in the end. A variety of Disney characters, as well as sound bites from a collection of classic Disney songs, resonate throughout the presentation.

The 25-minute show starts with Mickey perched on a darkened island, acting as a conductor. Music resounds and sprays of water "dance" around the island. Screens of water pop up and images, like Sorcerer Mickey from *Fantasia*, Simba and Nala from *The Lion King*, and undersea creatures from *The Little Mermaid*, are projected. Mickey's dream gets darker and more ominous as the show progresses, with many Disney villains making appearances.

While Disney's creative staff had to work Fantasmic! around existing landmarks at Disneyland, the folks who designed Fantasmic! at Hollywood Studios had no such impediments. They simply built a new arena, called the Hollywood Hills Amphitheater, behind the Theater of the Stars and Twilight Zone Tower of Terror off Sunset Boulevard. The new venue seats 6,900 guests, with enough room for 3,000 standees.

In front of the amphitheater is a moat, capable of holding 1.9 million gallons of water. Beyond the moat is a 50-foot-tall mountain where much of the action takes place. Where Disneyland uses the *Columbia* and the *Mark Twain*, Hollywood Studios employs a new 80-foot-long vessel modeled after the boat used in *Steamboat Willie*.

In deference to the often inclement weather in Florida, a four-minute-long substitute show, called Taste of Fantasmic!, is shown in place of the main show, keeping the 46 performers and the variety of show props from encountering dangerous conditions.

Like many shows in Disney parks, dining and desert packages are available, which means guests who partake of this perk will receive VIP seating for the performance.

Indiana Jones Epic Stunt Spectacular

Have you ever taken an adventure to Echo Lake,
Where your health and safety are at stake?

Where urchins and thieves are everywhere,
With only one brave hero to protect you there.

Professor Indiana Jones to be correct,
The finest antiquities locator since and yet.

Finding long-hidden treasures are rather easy,
But keeping them safe could make you queasy.

Yet, by the end of each show, Indy triumphs in glory,
With a spectacular end to each adventurous story.

GIVING STUNT PERFORMERS THEIR 'PROPS'

The thinking behind Disney-MGM Studios was to create a place where guests could get a behind-the-scenes look at how the magic is made.

One of the main attractions in the park when it opened in 1989 was the Indiana Jones Epic Stunt Spectacular, a theatrical presentation which thrust stunt performers into a place that they were unfamiliar with—namely, the spotlight.

Between earth-shattering crashes, realistic-looking fight scenes, and fiery explosions, a second-unit director serves as our host as he explains the ins and outs of how stunt professionals bring excitement and realism to some of the most iconic scenes from the blockbuster film *Raiders of the Lost Ark*. The stunt doubles of the movie's stars, Indiana Jones and Marion, also interact with the audience as they take us through one intense scene after another.

The show starts with Indy walking on stage and coming perilously close to "getting the point" as a series of long spears come shooting up from the ground. Unscathed, he reaches his goal—a golden idol perched atop a rock. He grabs the idol and replaces it with a bag of sand, but his actions trigger the release of a massive ball of stone, which comes rolling toward him. Indy runs away from it, but the stone overtakes him and seemingly crushes our hero as it does. After a few anxious seconds, though, Indy appears unscathed. A technician then walks onto the set and easily rolls the lightweight "stone" back to its perch, resetting it for the next show.

Other key sequences from *Raiders* are replicated, giving the audience a better understanding of just how elaborate stunts are and how important a role stunt professionals play.

There's a chaotic truck chase scene, which ends with a vehicle flipping over and bursting into flames, and a fight sequence where Indy and Marion are chased by German soldiers to the rooftops before they escape by jumping off the side of a building.

As the second-unit director talks to the audience between scene changes and explains what has happened and what to expect next, the massive sets (built atop large rolling platforms) are pulled into place by a tractor.

The grand finale of the show replicates the classic scene from the movie involving Indy, Marion, a hulking German soldier, and a spinning, propeller-driven airplane. It ends with Indy and Marion running from the plane in a hail of machine-gun fire before the plane bursts into flames. The heat from the explosion is so intense that it can be felt by the audience members.

It's a spectacular ending to a truly epic stunt presentation, one that gives stunt performers their "props."

The Drop Inn

Please drop in and say hello,
Perhaps someone's here that you may know.

Please drop in, and stay here for a while,
We are newly decorated in the latest style.

Our elevator will bring you to the proper floor,
It's located just behind the entrance door.

Take a seat and place all items beneath your chair,
You'll be more comfortable stowing them there.

We may bump into each other again some day,
I'm sure you'll remember me for forever and a day.

THE TWILIGHT ZONE TOWER OF TERROR

An attraction that plays into one of man's greatest fears—being stuck inside an elevator as it plummets toward the ground—was the genesis behind Twilight Zone Tower of Terror, which looms imposingly large at the end of Sunset Boulevard and can be seen for miles from outside Hollywood Studios.

The big difference between your average elevator in a typical office building and Twilight Zone Tower of Terror? Your Tower of Terror ride vehicle falls through its shaft faster than the speed of gravity—before going up and down, then up and down again and again in a series of frighteningly random drops. And...this Tower is haunted.

For Twilight Zone Tower of Terror, Disney's creative team put together the perfect blending of the ground-breaking 1960s television series, Disney's technical expertise, and the right amount of gut-wrenching, edge-of-your-seat thrills. As with every Disney attraction, the story is equally important as the ride itself. And Twilight Zone Tower of Terror has a compelling story to tell.

The attraction is set in the elegant Hollywood Tower Hotel during the late 1930s—October 31, 1939, to be exact. During a violent storm on that spooky evening, the hotel is struck by lightning, leading to the unexplained disappearance of five hotel guests who were on an elevator heading up to their rooms.

Fast-forward to the present. The now-abandoned Hollywood Tower Hotel dominates Hollywood Studios' Sunset Boulevard; indeed, as you make your way toward the attraction, the shrieks and screams of "delighted" guests as the doors open near the top of the building grab your attention.

What sets this attraction far apart from most others is the elaborate queue area. So much thought and detail went into the rooms leading up to the actual ride that you could literally spend hours checking out every nook and cranny. The hotel's lobby looks as it did on that fateful night in 1939—only, it's empty. It appears that everyone just got up and left. There's a newspaper on a table, a board game that's half finished, tea and pastries, old-fashioned luggage...and plenty of cobwebs.

On closer inspection, the lobby is a veritable Twilight Zone hall of fame, with memorabilia from many of the show's classic episodes used as well-placed props. For example, there's a book with the title "To Serve Man," so named for the classic episode when visitors from outer space landed on Earth (we thought they came here to serve us; in reality, they came here to bring Earthlings back to their planet to *eat us for dinner*).

Guests are escorted from the lobby to a library room, where a vintage black-and-white TV set suddenly turns on and our host, Rod Serling himself, introduces the next *Twilight Zone* episode. Actually, he says it's an episode that calls for a different kind of introduction. And *you* are about to become the star.

You're then led to the boiler room area of the building, where several service elevators—as well as some overly creepy bellhops—await to assist you to your room. Of course, when they ask you to sit on a bench inside the elevator and then make you fasten a safety belt, you quickly get the idea that this isn't going to be a normal elevator ride.

You're lifted uneventfully to the 13th floor, where the door opens and your elevator does something unlike any other elevator you've ever experienced—it exits the shaft and goes horizontally across a darkened corridor. As it turns out, your "elevator" is actually something called an autonomous guided vehicle, or AGV for short. You're being taken, all right—beyond sight and sound, shadow and substance, all the way to the fifth dimension.

It's here where shadowy apparitions of the five lost guests from the lightning storm nearly 80 years ago appear in the distance. If you look closely, the child in the group is clutching a Mickey Mouse doll. Just as quickly as they appear, they disappear, replaced by twinkling stars.

By now, first-time riders grab ever-so-tightly onto the handlebars and start to process exactly what they've experienced so far. They remember minutes before, standing outside the building, seeing people at the top, screaming their lungs out...and then watching as they plummet downward. They recall how they had just gone *up* an elevator shaft and were taken across the building to another shaft. What goes up, they begin the realize, must go...

The ride technology for Twilight Zone Tower of Terror was first proposed for a ride to be called Geyser Mountain in Disneyland Paris in the early 1990s. That ride never saw the light of day, but the proposed "drop shaft" concept was resurrected, refined, and put to use in the Hollywood Tower Hotel.

There are actually four ascent shafts inside the building, with a series of corridors leading the AGVs to the two drop shafts which you see in the front of the building. Once your AGV is positioned into the drop shaft, it's connected on top and bottom to heavy steel wires. For what seems like two eternities, you sit. And wait. And then...you drop.

In reality, your vehicle is pulled downward faster than the speed of gravity. That explains why many riders who have camera bags or jewelry around their necks will see those items float in front of their faces during the descents.

When Twilight Zone Tower of Terror opened on July 22, 1994, it had just one drop; the ride was over before you had a chance to lose your lunch. As the years went by—and the Disney Imagineers' imaginations got more and more twisted—several computer-generated random drop-and-lift sequences were added. At one point during the sequence, the doors slide open and the expanse of Hollywood Studios is spread out in front of you. Down and up and down again...until, mercifully, the vehicle reaches the bottom of the shaft and the exit doors open. But not before Rod Serling bids you all a chilling farewell.

The Tower of Terror attraction in Hollywood Studios remains the only ride themed to *The Twilight Zone*. The other tower attractions in Disney parks around the world have been re-imagined: they are now themed to Marvel's *Guardians of the Galaxy*.

Beauty and the Beast

Beauty and the Beast can rival shows on Broadway,
Arrive early to watch this stage show fantasy.
You'll learn that true beauty can only be found within,
Beauty has nothing to do with the outside of your skin.

A LIVE SHOW WITH THE
APPEAL OF BROADWAY

When Disney's creative team began developing a third theme park at Walt Disney World, to be known as Disney-MGM Studios, it did so with the idea that it would just be a half-day experience, nothing as elaborate as the Magic Kingdom or Epcot.

But as the planners sank their teeth into the project, they soon realized that the concept could be much more extensive, far greater than the initial proposal of giving guests just a behind-the-scenes look at movie and TV production. Attractions were added prior to opening, and others were put on the drawing board for the months post opening.

One of the elements added to the Studios' now growing mix of entertainment options was the idea of presenting live stage shows, giving guests a show that rivaled a Broadway production. Since theatrical venues weren't in the original construction plans, Disney had to wing it during the first few years of operation. Temporary venues were set up, one near the Hollywood Brown Derby restaurant, just off what became Sunset Boulevard, the other to the rear of the park, behind New York Street.

At these temporary sites, Disney-MGM Studios presented a series of live stage shows based on hit animated films released during the time. Beauty and the Beast: Live on Stage ran from 1991–1993 at the Brown Derby site, then was moved to the New York Street area (known as the Backlot Theater), where it ran from 1993–1994 as Sunset Boulevard was being constructed. Also on the site near New York Street, The Spirit of Pocahontas was staged from 1995–1996, followed by The Hunchback of Notre Dame: A Musical Adventure, from 1996–2002.

In 1994, Sunset Boulevard opened as a new "land" in the Studios, anchored by Twilight Zone Tower of Terror and the Theater of the Stars, which would be the permanent home of Beauty and the Beast: Live on Stage. Theater of the Stars was inspired by some of the country's most noteworthy outdoor amphitheaters, among them the Hollywood Bowl.

The Beauty and the Beast theatrical production at Hollywood Studios stays true to the animated classic, following a similar storyline and using many of the film's most beloved songs. The seating and stage areas are covered, but the theater is not air-conditioned.

Muppet Vision 3-D

Kermit the Frog and Dr. Bunsen Honeydew,
Have a very exciting show in store for you.

There are so many friends to stop in and see,
The amazing entertainment with Bean Bunny.

Of course, the famous Swedish Chef and Gonzo,
Miss Piggy, and Fozzie Bear, will be there, too.

Come over to Grand Avenue and stop in to see,
The super fabulous show Muppets show in 3-D.

THE SHORT-LIVED DISNEY-JIM HENSON RELATIONSHIP

In recent years, the Walt Disney Company and several major franchises in the world of entertainment have joined forces.

There were Disney's much-heralded acquisitions of Marvel Comics and Lucasfilms and the working agreement with James Cameron to build Pandora: The World of Avatar, based on Cameron's wildly successful film *Avatar*, in Disney's Animal Kingdom.

And then there was the short-lived Disney-Jim Henson alliance, forged in 1989.

"I grew up on the Disney movies," said Henson, the man who created the Muppets, *Sesame Street*, and the Teenage Mutant Ninja Turtles, among a host of other successful projects. "Every new animated feature was a major event in my upbringing. And the parks have always been among my favorite places. The idea of designing for them is a wonderful thing to me. The first film I saw was *Snow White* and ever since then, I've had a secret desire to work with this great company."

At the time of the prospective merger, Disney CEO Michael Eisner said: "Just about every newspaper in the country featured our joining with the Muppets as if it were a merger of GM and Ford Motor Company." For his part, Henson said joining forces with Disney was "a deal so natural it's more like a marriage than a merger."

That "marriage" was sealed with a handshake between Eisner and Henson after a breakfast meeting. To both men (especially Henson), that was enough to cement the agreement. An enthusiastic Henson began working on all the new and exciting Muppet-themed attractions he'd bring to the Disney fold, preferring to let the lawyers sort out all the details of the merger later on.

Henson, of course, died unexpectedly in May 1990 before his production company and Disney could formally dot all the i's and cross all the t's and the much-heralded Mickey-Muppets deal fell through in the months after his death. Henson's children ran their dad's company for more than a decade before selling the rights to the Muppets and Bear in the Big Blue House to Disney in 2004.

A number of projects, already in the works when Henson died, saw the light of day in 1990, among them "The Muppets at Walt Disney World" (a special episode of *The Magical World of Disney* TV series) and live stage shows at Disney-MGM Studios ("Hollywood/Hollywood!" and "Here Come the Muppets" among them) as well as a full-scale presence in Disney parks parades.

The Muppet*Vision 3-D attraction, still quite popular in what is now known as Disney's Hollywood Studios, was in production when Henson died. The show debuted on May 16, 1991, on the one-year anniversary of Henson's death.

There were several other projects planned for the Muppets which were scrapped and added to the list of Disney parks attractions that never saw the light of day. They included the Great Muppet Movie Ride (a takeoff of the Great Movie Ride attraction, starring Audio-Animatronics versions of the Muppets) and Great Gonzo's Pandemonium Pizza Parlor (presumably on the site of Mama Melrose's Italian restaurant, located right across the plaza from the Muppet*Vision 3-D theater).

Muppet*Vision 3-D is a madcap adventure which begins with Kermit the Frog guiding park guests on a tour of the Muppet Studios, where Kermit's fellow Muppets set up a demonstration of 3-D film technology. The tour unravels when Dr. Bunsen Honeydew's experimental sprite, Waldo, gets loose and causes chaos for Kermit, Miss Piggy, and the rest of the gang.

In typical tongue-in-cheek fashion, Disney's Imagineers placed a net full of Jello in the queue—a not-so-subtle reference to *Mickey Mouse Club* star Annette Funicello.

Star Tours: The Adventures Continue

Scan your wrist, you are on your way,
To be transported through the galaxy today.

Your fellow passengers are Ewoks and Droids,
Jedi knights, storm troopers, and girls and boys.

You may experience turbulence along the way,
So, finish eating before entering the departure bay.

Our transporter will spin around and twirl,
Making you feel like a disoriented squirrel.

If you're brave, this could be your best ride ever
So, buckle up, you're about to begin a new endeavor.

A Galaxy Far, Far Away

Zoom though the universe at an unheard of pace,
To locations somewhere inside of outer space.

You will see droids and robots of every kind,
Trying their best to defeat an evil mastermind.

So, buckle up and begin your unique adventure,
Star Tours...every moment becomes a treasure.

SPEEDING THROUGH THE
STAR WARS GALAXY

When Star Tours debuted in Disneyland in 1987 and
Walt Disney World in 1989, it represented a radical
departure for Disney: an attraction that wasn't based on
a Disney-created film.

The phenomenal popularity of the Star Wars
films inspired Disney to join forces with the series'
creator, George Lucas, for an attraction, to be based in
Tomorrowland in Disneyland and Disney-MGM Studios
in WDW. Lucas had worked with Disney previously on
Captain EO, which starred Michael Jackson. (Years later,
Lucas would sell the rights to Star Wars to Disney, pre-
senting a new world of opportunities for the extremely
popular movie franchise.)

Disney first conceived of a flight simulator attraction
in the late 1970s, based on the movie *The Black Hole*. The
high cost of the attraction, as well as the tepid response
to the movie, forced Disney to cancel the project.

But when Disney and Lucas' Industrial Light and Magic
(ILM) and Lucasfilm Ltd. decided to collaborate on a Star
Wars-themed attraction, to be named Star Tours, the idea
of an attraction using a flight simulator was resurrected.

Star Tours evolved into a 3-D adventure that took 40
guests on a break-neck ride through the Star Wars uni-
verse, culminating with a thrilling chase through the
outer corridors of the notorious Death Star.

At the entrance of the WDW Star Tours attraction, there's a giant replica of an AT-AT standing guard. The building and the surrounding environs take on the appearance of a woodsy Ewok village. Once inside, the winding queue area shows off a life-size StarSpeeder 1000, the vehicle that will take us on our intergalactic adventure. There also are a wide assortment of droids on display, including C-3PO and R2-D2, to amuse and entertain guests as they made their way to the boarding area.

On board the StarSpeeder during the original version of the adventure, seat-belted guests were introduced to Rex, their reluctant pilot (voiced by Pee Wee Herman). The premise of the attraction saw guests, who had signed up for a routine sightseeing tour, thrust into a perilous quest to protect a Rebel spy from the Galactic Empire.

To Rex's chagrin, the StarSpeeder unexpectedly takes off and begins hurtling over, under, around, and through several intergalactic obstacles. After gaining his bearings, Rex announces: "Light speed to Endor!" and the StarSpeeder jolts into hyper-speed. As guests viewed the action on a screen at the front of the vehicle, the StarSpeeder itself rocked side-to-side and back-and-forth in conjunction with the film, enhancing the sensation of motion.

Star Tours was re-imagined in 2011 and was renamed Star Tours: The Adventures Continue. The updated version includes scenes from the most recent Star Wars movies and features enhanced digital capabilities. In addition, the new version takes travelers to a myriad of locations from the Star Wars universe, including Naboo, Tatooine, Hoth, Kashyyk, and Coruscant.

To add to the excitement, Disney and LucasFilms incorporated more than 50 different scene combinations, ensuring that each flight will be a different adventure. Included in the mix is a pod race on Tatooine, a speeder pursuit on Kashyyk, and an underwater submarine chase on Naboo.

After the white-knuckle five-minute flight, the pilot manages to return the StarSpeeder and its passengers safely to a spaceport.

Star Tours: The Adventures Continue will be joined by a variety of Star Wars-themed attractions in 2019 when a new land, Star Wars: On Galaxy's Edge, opens in Hollywood Studios.

CHAPTER FOUR

Disney's Animal Kingdom

A Festival Celebrating 'The Lion King'

A whirlwind of magic is about to begin,
Roar like a lion if they're your new kin.

Baa as loud as you can if you're a giraffe,
Use your deepest voice and try not to laugh.

If you are chosen to become a warthog,
They sound like a bull or an angry watchdog.

My favorite animal is the elephant,
There just like me...gentle and intelligent.

Enjoy the animal you are chosen to be,
Then enjoy the show; it's as good as can be.

Animal Kingdom

Exotic animals roam lush African savannahs,
While small monkeys eat oranges and fresh bananas.

Pocahontas tells us a story in Grandma Willow's Grove,
As her friends contently crawl below or fly above.

Spinning roller-coasters rapidly twist and twirl,
Primeval Whirl is a favorite ride for any boy or girl.

Go on Kilimanjaro Safaris to see some elephants,
A day at Animal Kingdom is a day of excellence.

Animal Kingdom Surprise

Surprise the grandkids with a magical vacation,
Starting out with a train ride to Harambe Station.

Charles, Janet, Kylie, Henry, and Ginny,
All loved to visit Camp Mickey-Minnie.

Richard, Robert, Lenny, and Lee,
Think that Pandora is the best place to be.

Gregg, Cavrel, Kristian, and Vinny,
Run off to join an African safari.

Vincent and Jacob love Affection Section,
While Abigail and Amelia adore Conservation Station.

Tracy, Kelly, Taresa, and Theresa,
Can't wait to ride on the Primeval twister.

Ryan and Aaron like to arrive as early as can be,
To see It's Tough to Be a Bug! inside the big tree.

Animal Kingdom is a favorite place to be,
For everyone in our entire family.

A Vegan in a Kingdom of Animals

It's difficult to stay vegan or vegetarian,
When your family goes away on vacation.

But it's no problem in the Animal Kingdom,
There is plenty to choose from, in my opinion.

Everywhere you look there's fruits and vegetables,
Not to mention pineapple whip and warm, tasty pretzels.

Just about every restaurant offers vegan delights,
My favorites are lettuce salad and whole grain rice.

There is no need for you to pack a sandwich or two,
There are numerous vegan choices available for you.

DISNEY'S ANIMAL KINGDOM
BROKE NEW GROUND

When CEO Michael Eisner tasked the members of Walt Disney Imagineering to design a park that was centered around animals, they were going where no entertainment company had ever gone before.

It's no wonder that it took 10 years, from 1980 until the park opened in 1989, for Disney's design team to bring the ambitious project to fruition. During that time, a core group of designers, headed by Joe Rohde, conducted several boots-on-the-ground trips around the world to do research, collect samples, make drawings, take photos, and immerse themselves in cultures and traditions that they would replicate in the eclectic new park.

What they came up with was a park that is perhaps the most unique, authentic experience you can find in any theme park setting.

The philosophy behind Animal Kingdom is something Disney calls "edu-tainment": educating guests, while entertaining them. There also is an unwavering sense of conservationism that permeates the park, in hopes that people who visit will bring back what they've learned and apply it to their everyday lives back home.

When Animal Kingdom opened on April 22, 1989, it consisted of the Oasis entry portal; Safari Village, the park's hub; Africa; Conservation Station; DinoLand USA; and Camp Minnie-Mickey. A land devoted to Asia was still under construction on opening day.

Safari Village houses the incredible Tree of Life, the park's stunning icon, where 325 carved animals can be seen on its massive trunk. DinoLand USA's main attraction on opening day was Countdown to Extinction, a dark thrill ride back millions of years to rescue an endangered Iguanodon. Africa, meanwhile, featured a stunning replica of an East African coastal village and also served as the entryway to the Kilimanjaro Safaris attraction, which took guests on an exciting trip through a vast savannah, populated by scores of live animals and a lush landscape that took years to assemble and grow. Indeed, Animal Kingdom has plants from every continent on Earth, except Antarctica. Finally, Conservation Station served to embody all that Animal Kingdom stood for, namely, conserving and protecting all of Earth's vast and wonderful creatures.

About a year after Animal Kingdom opened, Asia was expanded with the Maharajah Jungle Trek and Kali River Rapids, an exciting raft ride with a message. In 2006, Asia was expanded once again when it introduced the thrilling Expedition Everest roller-coaster and the accompanying village of Serka Zong. The perilous mountain adventure gave Animal Kingdom a signature, E-ticket attraction, as well as a landmark that was visible from miles away.

Most of the other lands in the park have received significant upgrades over the years. One land, however, was torn down in 2015 to make way for what has become the talk of Walt Disney World. Camp Minnie-Mickey, themed after an Adirondack resort in upstate New York, was an original land in the park, but save for the Festival of the Lion King show, was not all that popular. When Disney struck a deal with *Avatar* creator James Cameron, the Festival of the Lion King show was moved to Africa and construction began on what it now known as Pandora: The World of Avatar, which opened to rave reviews in May 2017.

The new land immerses guests in the world of Pandora and introduces us to its native inhabitants, the Na'vi. It features a stunning re-creation of the fabled floating mountains from the film, as well as glowing, bio-luminescent highlights and realistic-looking foliage from Pandora.

Disney's creative staff, with Cameron's Lightstorm Entertainment Co., dreamed up two attractions for the new land. There's the Na'vi River Journey, which takes guests on a gentle boat ride through a lush Pandoran rainforest, with many of the movie's native creatures peeking out from behind leaves and branches. The ride culminates with a viewing of the Shaman of Song, one of the most advanced Audio-Animatronics figures Disney has ever come up with. And then there's the Avatar: Flight of Passage attraction, a mega-hit from the day it opened that still sees wait times exceeding three hours.

Flight of Passage delivers an immersive adventure like no other: you experience just what it's like to fly on the back of a banshee. You soar through Pandora, dodging tree limbs, floating mountains, a breaching whale-like creature, and other banshees. You soar up into the clouds... and straight down a mountain cliff. As you do, your link chair "breathes" under you and a variety of sensory cues enhance an experience that is truly exhilarating.

Pandora: The World of Avatar was the latest attempt by Disney to make Animal Kingdom more enticing after the sun goes down. In Asia, the colorful and inspiring Rivers of Light show wows guests with a broad mix of sights and sounds, Kilimanjaro Safaris offers an entirely new perspective on the animals who populate the savannah, and the Tree of Life hosts an imaginative projection show.

On April 22, 2018, Disney's Animal Kingdom celebrated its 20th anniversary, wildly fulfilling the hopes and dreams of the creative staff who helped bring this unique theme park adventure to life.

Expedition Everest

If you are a fearless human that's forty-four inches or taller,
You can delve into a place of amazement and wonder.

Beware of the hazardous spaces that are always forbidden,
In this vast expanse where many dangers could be hidden.

It's been said the Abominable Snowman could be near,
And this strange Himalayan creature can sense your fear.

Be advised you may only succeed if you're the cleverest,
On your memorable expedition to the summit of Mount Everest.

TAKING ROLLER-COASTERS
TO NEW HEIGHTS

Things were so much simpler during the early days of roll-er-coaster design. To begin with, the early roller-coasters were always outdoors, meaning there were few limits on the coasters' designers in terms of size or length. And they were always wooden, with steel tracks. The cars on the coaster track also used steel wheels to increase speed. At the beginning of the ride, motors connected to a drive train or cable would raise the coaster train to the highest point of the track, and then gravity would take over, hurtling the train down and then up a series of shorter elevations, with assorted curves mixed in to enhance the experience. One of the main drawbacks of this design method was you could only put a single train on the track at a time, to avoid the possibility of one train catching up to and colliding with another.

Roller-coasters can be traced back to the heyday of coal mines, where ore buckets on steel tracks stretched for miles inside mines. Coal companies would allow adventurous types to ride in the buckets—for a fee, of course. Perhaps the most famous early roller-coaster was the Cyclone in Coney Island in the New York City borough of Brooklyn, which opened in 1927. Although the Cyclone attained legendary status, the popularity of roller coasters, in general, declined during the Depression years.

In the late 1950s, Walt Disney visited the set of his company's movie *Third Man on the Mountain*, which took place on the Matterhorn in the Swiss Alps. Thus inspired, Disney returned to the United States with a bold idea for a new attraction at Disneyland: a roller-coaster with tracks that ran mostly inside a replica of the Matterhorn. Imagineer Bob Gurr was given the daunting task (remember, he didn't have computers to fall back on) of putting not one, but two roller-coaster tracks weaving inside and outside of the faux mountain. Working alongside members of Arrow Development, the team opted to use tubular steel for the track—an industry first—which allowed for more flexibility in the course design. They also came up with something that was dubbed a "booster brake."

"The Matterhorn has little rotating wheels at the crest of the hills," Gurr said. "This was an invention by Arrow Development. If the roller-coaster car was going too slow at the top of a hill, the rotating wheels would boost the car ahead. Or if the car was going too fast, it would slow it down. That's why we called it a booster brake." The system allowed Disney to do something that had never been done before when it came to roller-coasters: put more than one train on the track at the same time.

Of course, Disney enhanced the overall Matterhorn experience by adding a story to the attraction: inside the mountain, lurking behind icy grottos and waterfalls, was the figure of the Abominable Snowman.

Fast forward to 2003, when Disney announced its plans to revisit the idea of a mythical creature hidden inside a legendary mountain that can only be seen while riding a roller-coaster.

The Asia section of Animal Kingdom was selected to house the thrilling new attraction Expedition Everest: Legend of the Forbidden Mountain. It took more than three years to research, design, and build the coaster and the replica of Mount Everest. More than 38 miles of rebar was used in building the mountain, along with, 1,800 tons of structural steel and 10,000 tons of concrete. The Forbidden Mountain is almost 200 feet tall, making it the tallest of the 18 man-made Disney-themed mountains worldwide.

What makes this attraction so appealing to coaster aficionados is that a portion of the ride goes backwards into the darkened center of the mountain. Once the runaway train grinds to a halt, it speeds forward again, this time out of the mountain and down an 80-foot drop.

After a series of breakneck curves, the train re-enters the mountain and encounters its: the ferocious Yeti.

As with everything Disney does, a tremendous amount of detail went into the overall design of Expedition Everest and the expansive queue area. Among the sights you'll see before boarding the Anandapur Rail Service (aka the roller-coaster) is the village of Serka Zong, which serves as a place-setter for the story of the Yeti. There's a museum dedicated to the Yeti, a tea garden, a room filled with mountain climbing equipment, and a temple featuring holy figures.

Expedition Everest, the most expensive roller-coaster ever built, opened on April 7, 2006.

Wild Africa Trek

Do not forget to bring your courage and your camera,
To visit the Safari River in Animal Kingdom's Africa.
Safari guides will lead you on a three-hour tour,
To visit the wildlife with adventures galore.
Trackers will guide you safely through the valley,
If you adhere to their directions and don't dilly-dally.
Or you can insist they do everything your way,
Your guides will return for you before sunset the next day.

TAKING A WALK ON THE WILD SIDE

The Walt Disney Company has its own nomenclature when it comes to its employees. First and foremost, those employees are referred to as cast members. Their work uniforms are called costumes. When they report to work, they are part of the show. When they're working, the cast members are onstage. When they leave their posts, they are headed backstage, where regular guests are prohibited.

When Disney's Animal Kingdom introduced Wild Africa Trek in 2011, it was with the express intent of giving Disney guests the ultimate backstage experience.

Wild Africa Trek, which requires a separate fee, is a unique, behind-the-scenes wildlife encounter and is in keeping with Animal Kingdom's goal of bringing together people and animals. It also bolsters the park's reputation as a venue that regularly introduces adventures that are a cut above anything you can find in a typical theme park.

During Wild Africa Trek, small groups of up to 12 adventurous souls embark on a three-hour, expert-led walk through some of the unexplored, off-the-beaten-path areas of Animal Kingdom's massive wildlife preserve. You hike through areas thick with bushes and branches, pesky roots, and underbrush. The guide leading the group explains what to expect along the way, while the guide bringing up the rear encourages any stragglers to forge ahead.

Before you even head out onto the trail, you receive some pre-trek instructions on safety. You're given canteens for water and sturdy vests with carabiners attached to them. Then it's off on the adventure of a lifetime.

The first stop along the wooded trail is an overlook. In the waterway below is an area where giant hippos congregate. At this point, the guides clip your carabiner to a steel wire and you can now walk out to the edge of the overlook to get a closer view of the 3,000-plus pound creatures who spend a good portion of their day underwater.

From here it's on to one of the highlights of the experience: a trip across a wobbly, 150-foot long rope bridge that dangles precariously some 50 feet above the hippo area you had just visited. You climb up steps to an observation tower, where the guides clip the carabiners to a steel wire above that stretches the length of the bridge, and then, one by one, trekkers grab hold of the rope on either side and head out onto the now swaying bridge. The planks below are unevenly spaced, some by as much as two feet apart, and every so often, there's a broken plank.

Your goal is to get to the other side, where another wooden observation deck awaits. There's no turning back from here, as another 150-foot rope bridge needs to be navigated before you reach the safety of firm, dry land. This bridge is a tad more foreboding as you soon realize that underneath you are at least a dozen large and menacing Nile crocodiles. Since you're always looking down to make sure you make it safely to the next plank, it's hard to miss the imposing, steel-gray bodies below.

Once the group has completed its unforgettable journey across the rope bridges, they can observe the crocs from another overlook area. From there, it's a short walk to a loading dock, where a flatbed truck awaits to take you out onto the vast savannah. The truck has comfortable benches and plenty of room to stand and walk around. They even supply guests with field glasses, to get a better view of the savannah's stunning assortment of wild animals. The truck follows the standard Kilimanjaro Safaris trail, with one big difference: your driver will pull over to give trekkers additional time to observe the animals, many of whom are not shy about walking within a few feet of the truck.

The truck then makes its way to the highest point in the savannah, where a little slice of civilization awaits—a private safari camp. It features a covered observation deck on which guests can relax and look out onto the savannah below. There also are clean bathrooms. Lunch—a tempting selection of African delicacies in a three-tiered tin—is served here as well.

After lunch, it's back out onto the safari trail before the trek comes to an end, although the memories gained during the experience are sure to last a lifetime.

Conservation Station

At Rafiki's Planet Watch, Doc McStuffins
Will teach you about animals and their customs.
The best part is if you are in a wheelchair like me,
You can roll around anywhere you'd like to be.

If you kindly wash your hands before and after,
You can pet animals and listen for Rafiki's laughter.
Watch small and large animals while they are at play,
A visit to Conservation Station will ensure a wonderful day.

CONSERVATION STATION: THE HEART OF ANIMAL KINGDOM'S MISSION

Conservation Station is located far off the beaten path at Disney's Animal Kingdom, on the outskirts of Africa, and is accessible only by train (the Wildlife Express). Yet, in a real sense, Conservation Station is at the heart of everything the park embraces.

The Walt Disney Company and animals have been unmistakably intertwined since the days of animated shorts, Oswald the Lucky Rabbit, and Mickey Mouse. Even after Disney transitioned into full-length animated feature films, animals often were the headliners. In the late 1940s, Walt stepped away from the world of animated creatures and championed a series of film documentaries that told the stories of a variety of species in the wild.

He contracted filmmakers Alfred and Elma Milotte for the project. They headed to Alaska's Pribilof Islands to capture wild animals in their natural habitats. The result was the Academy Award-winning documentary *Seal Island*, which launched the successful True-Life Adventures series and, in turn, kick-started Disney's commitment to environmental and animal conservation.

When Disney CEO Michael Eisner gave the green light in the early 1980s to create an animal-themed park, he did so with the understanding that the park would be a champion for animals, particularly endangered species. Although many of the attractions in the park would tell stories with strong conservation themes, Conservation Station would be "the real heart of the message at Animal Kingdom," according to Disney Imagineer and show writer Paula Kessler.

A large, brightly colored montage of animals and bird faces greets guests as they approach Conservation Station's main building. Inside the building, in the Hall of Animals, hundreds of animal faces are pictured on a curved mural, staring down at the human guests. According to former facility curator Dr. Jackie Ogden, "The animals are looking *at* you and *to* you—the human species—for man represents both the greatest danger to the animals and their environment and their greatest hope for survival."

Throughout Conservation Station, there are demonstrations and educational tools that, it's hoped, will inspire visitors to learn about animal care and conservation, and perhaps more importantly, motivate them to return home and take a more active role in animal welfare causes.

According to Zofia Kostyrko, one of the park's original designers, "Our show is for children and children-at-heart, to arouse their emotional feelings for animals by showing the beauty and richness of the animal kingdom."

While inside the area, which is now known as Rafiki's Planet Watch, guests get to witness first-hand as veterinarians work on animals, everything ranging from routine checkups to surgical procedures.

Also included in the experience is an area called Affection Section, where guests get to touch, pet, and interact with a variety of rare, domesticated animals and have their questions answered by the animal care experts who supervise them. As an added attraction, Disney Junior star Doc McStuffins often joins in on the fun.

Festival of the Lion King

Animal Kingdom's Festival of the Lion King
Is a marvelous place for you to dance and sing.
You'll see a royal prince and princess stroll by
As monkeys summersault nearly up to the sky.

Learn the way that wild jungle animals act,
And listen carefully as not to miss an important fact.
Make noise and act as the animal that you prefer to be,
Hakuna matata, no worries, it's so good to be free.

A MOVABLE FESTIVAL
CELEBRATING THE KING OF BEASTS

The Festival of the Lion King show is one of the few Disney theme park attractions that has been moved, not only from one venue to another, but from a different section of the park, as well.

Festival of the Lion King was an opening-day attraction when Animal Kingdom debuted on April 22, 1998. It was the main draw in the Camp Minnie-Mickey section of the park and, indeed, was one of the most popular attractions in the entire Animal Kingdom. The Broadway-style production features singers, dancers, acrobats, stilt-walkers and Audio-Animatronics figures in a grand celebration centered around the story of *The Lion King*, the hit animated movie released in 1994.

When it opened, Festival of The Lion King was staged in a rustic, open-air amphitheater that was reminiscent of an upstate New York summer theater. After several steamy years, the venue was enclosed and air-conditioned. Although the venue seated 1,000 guests, most were in close proximity to the center of the theater, where much of the action took place. That seating area was divided into four sections, each with its own distinctive name—lion, giraffe, warthog, and elephant. Guests in each section took part in a rousing pre-show where they were encouraged to make sounds similar to the animals their section was named for, which resulted in some hilarious grunting and snorting sounds.

Each section of the theater was bi-sected by four tracks. On these tracks, four rolling stages would enter the theater from backstage as the show began.

Audio-Animatronics figures from the movie—Simba, an elephant, two swaying giraffe heads, and Timon and Pumbaa—were propped atop the four stages.

Performers in colorful African tribal costumes opened the show with "I Just Can't Wait to be King." A group known as the Tumble Monkeys then made their way to center stage. The brightly dressed "primates" were world-class gymnasts in disguise. With "Hakuna Matata" blasting over the loudspeakers, the monkeys bounced playfully on trampolines and swung from ropes, as if they actually had no worries. Other highlights included tribal warriors on stilts performing "Be Prepared," as well as giant bird-like devices and high-flying aerialists. The rousing finale, which included the entire cast, featured stirring renditions of "The Lion Sleeps Tonight" and "The Circle of Life."

The high quality of the show and its performers often elicited responses of "thrilling" and "exhilarating" from joyful guests after each performance.

When Disney and filmmaker James Cameron joined forces to create a new land in Animal Kingdom based on the mega-hit movie *Avatar*, Camp Minnie-Mickey became expendable. It was decided that Pandora: The World of Avatar would take up residence where Camp Minnie-Mickey once stood, and all of that land's attractions—except one—would be scrapped. Festival of The Lion King was deemed too popular to close, so a new theater, located in the Africa section of the park, was constructed to give the show a new, permanent venue in an area of the park that was more suited to its storyline.

The Tree of Life

One hundred and forty-five feet tall,
And a total amazement for all.

A handsome horned rhinoceros,
And an attractive hippopotamus.

A dangerous lion and a slinky scorpion,
Near a playful monkey and a docile dolphin.
There are too many animals to name them all,
Some fly, some walk and some even crawl.
A tortoise, a lemur, an eagle, and a bear,
Stop to see them the next time you're there.

A PARK'S ICON TAKES ROOT

Think it's easy to design a theme park? Consider this fact: it took almost 10 years from the time Disney's Animal Kingdom was first conceived to the day it opened its gates in 1998. During that nearly one decade of planning, so much went into the design and development of the park. First, the planners had to come up with an overriding theme (the story of animals, past, present, and mythical). Then, they needed to come up with ideas for shows and attractions centered around that theme. Of course, there was the added responsibility of just how to care for the nearly 1,700 animals from 250 species housed across the 500-plus acres of property.

As with other Disney parks, the planners had to settle on a central icon, something that would embody Animal Kingdom's mission of education and conservation. They settled on a tree. But not just any tree. It would be a man-made, 145-foot tall Tree of Life. They modeled it after one particular bonsai tree that was discovered during a trip to the International Flower & Garden Festival at Epcot.

The key component of the massive tree was its equally massive trunk. Carved into that trunk are animals—325 of them. It took 365 days for Imagineer Zsolt Hormay and his 10-person team to create the stunning work of art on the 50-foot-wide trunk. In addition, there are more than 102,000 man-made leaves on the tree, attached to more than 8,000 branches.

Since hurricanes and fierce winds are an issue in central Florida for six months out of the year, the Tree of Life had to be structurally solid in its design. Disney's planners opted to use the same principles used in building an oil rig when they designed the tree.

At one point, designers were planning to make the tree a walk-up attraction, where guests could view Animal Kingdom from nearly 200 feet high.

It took some time before the designers settled on how to make the best use of the space in the underbelly of the tree. At first, a walkthrough, similar to Cinderella Castle in the Magic Kingdom, was proposed. Then, a dining space—tentatively called the Roots Restaurant—was on the drawing board. But those concepts were scrapped.

It wasn't until CEO Michael Eisner floated the idea of putting an attraction under the Tree of Life that the It's Tough to Be a Bug! show was conceived.

Harambe Station

Travel with me on holiday to Harambe Station,
Taking the express train on our magical vacation.
We'll bring ponchos to protect us from a storm,
And purchase safari hats in case it gets warm.
Let's stop to buy souvenirs for both you and me,
Our camera will take photos of everything we see.
Delicious drinks made from tangerine and Sparberry,
Can be purchased at the nearby Wanjohi commissary.
For seldom-taken adventures it's best to be prepared,
Nothing is better than traveling on a train that's open-aired.
We can roam through Africa and Asia at our freedom,
I'm so happy we're spending time in the Animal Kingdom.

RECREATING AN EAST AFRICAN VILLAGE, DOWN TO THE SMALLEST DETAIL

When Disney's Animal Kingdom park guests cross over the stone bridge from Discovery Island and into the village of Harambe, they are walking into a true work of art.

Harambe, the hub in the Africa section of the park, is modeled after a typical coastal village in East Africa. What strikes guests as they enter the village is the incredible level of detail. Even though Harambe was brand new when Animal Kingdom opened its gates in 1998, it had the appearance of having been there for decades. In fact, the entire village looks tattered and weather-beaten, more makeshift than rock-solid. You'll notice rusted bicycles parked at the sides of buildings, bricks exposed because the stucco has begun to break down, faded signs touting local businesses. There's even a giant baobab tree on the outskirts of town, leading guests to Africa's main attraction, Kilimanjaro Safaris.

Appearances, however, can be deceiving. Getting Harambe to look old and run-down is an art form. Disney's designers walked a fine line between making the area look old and dilapidated while adhering to Florida's strict building codes. They also not only made certain elements *look* authentic, they actually *are* authentic. For example, the thatched roofs on the village's buildings were put together by 13 Zulu craftsmen who made three separate trips to the site. They constructed the roofs out of materials (hand-harvested Berg thatching grass and battens made from eucalyptus wood) shipped in from Africa. The thatched roofs not only look great, they are durable and can be expected to last upwards of 60 years.

Harambe boasts a wide assortment of dining options that give guests a true taste of African cuisine. There's Tusker House, a lavishly detailed restaurant that's home to one of Walt Disney World's most popular character buffets. There's also Harambe Market (African-style ribs, chicken, sausages, corn dogs, and beer), Tamu Tamu Refreshments (Dole Whip and a variety of desserts and beverages), Dawa Bar, Harambe Fruit Market, and Zuri's Sweets Shop. Kusafiri Coffee Shop and Bakery specializes in breakfast offerings.

Part of the lure of Harambe is its live—and lively—entertainment. Dancers and musicians, decked out in colorful African-inspired clothing, perform regularly, drawing enthusiastic crowds to Harambe's town square.

The most popular entertainment venue within Harambe's confines, however, is the Festival of the Lion King showplace. It's here, using puppets, Audio-Animatronics figures, and live singers, dancers, and acrobats, where a rousing celebration takes place several times during the day. The show features many of the movie's most popular songs, written by Elton John and Tim Rice, all leading up to a rousing rendition of "The Circle of Life."

The Boneyard

Bring your youngsters on over to the Boneyard,
To enjoy fossil fun, reservations are not required.

There are prehistoric puzzles just waiting to be solved,
It's even fun for toddlers because nothing is too involved.

Kids wander in search of a giant Tyrannosaurus rex,
While their parents enjoy some much-needed rest.

CAN YOU DIG IT? AT THE BONEYARD, YOU CAN.

Many youngsters love digging in the dirt. Still others love spending time in a playground. And just as many youngsters are fascinated by dinosaurs.

Put those three activities together and—voila!—you have the Boneyard, a rambling, open-air dig site set in the DinoLand USA section of Disney's Animal Kingdom.

Near the entrance of DinoLand USA and the Boneyard is a fitting landmark, setting the scene for all would-be paleontologists: Dino-Sue, an exact replica of the largest Tyrannosaurus rex skeleton ever found. Dino-Sue stands 13 feet tall and is 40 feet long. The original, on display at a museum in Chicago, is 67 million years old.

The Boneyard gives children the opportunity to search for dinosaur fossils, climb on the back of a partially unearthed skeleton, or just run around and burn off steam. Thankfully, Disney's designers filled the entire area with sand, thus avoiding kids returning to their parents caked in mud.

In the covered paleontological dig site, a combination of the partial skeletal remains of a Triceratops, a Tyrannosaurus rex and a woolly mammoth—all carved by Disney Imagineering sculptors—are there for the exploring.

To get to the dig site, youngsters must navigate a cushioned play area. From there, they climb up and over a scaffold bridge (dubbed the Olden Gate Bridge) and begin hunting for skeletons and fossils.

There are plaques scattered around the dig site that tell us what paleontologists are looking for as well as how they study their findings.

It's a chance for kids to learn as they play, one of the original and most important tenets of Animal Kingdom.

Flight of Passage

Fly on the back of a mountain banshee,
Look down below, there's so much to see.

Soon you'll be soaring above Pandora's fifth moon,
Hold on tightly or you may fall to your doom.

Your bravery combined with common sense and knowledge,
could glean amazing courage that will surely astonish.

Stay calm but alert and learn everything you can,
All that you see could be saved or destroyed by a single man.

SOARIN' ON THE BACK OF A BANSHEE

The centerpiece of Pandora: The World of Avatar is Flight of Passage, an "E-ticket attraction that allows guests to soar on a banshee over a vast alien world. The spectacular flying experience gives guests a bird's-eye view of the beauty and grandeur of the world of Pandora on an aerial rite of passage," said Imagineer Diego Parris.

The new land, based on the blockbuster movie *Avatar*, opened in 2017 to rave reviews. In addition to spectacular re-creations of the Floating Mountains as seen in the movie, there are two featured attractions: Flight of Passage and the Na'vi River Journey, a boat ride through a bioluminescent world of sights, sounds, and brilliant colors.

Flight of Passage borrows from the Soarin' simulated hang-gliding experience that has been thrilling guests at Epcot since 2006. Unlike Soarin', where rows of seats are hoisted up to 65 feet into the air and then positioned in front of a gigantic domed screen, on Flight of Passage guests enter the queue area and walk, almost imperceptibly, up a gradual incline. By the time they've boarded their "link chair," the ride vehicle, they've reached the necessary elevation without realizing it.

In simplest terms, Flight of Passage allows guests to experience what it feels like to fly while seated on the back of a banshee. The experience begins in the queue, which is about one-third of a mile long. The show building itself is an abandoned RDA (the human-run Resources Development Administration) facility. Along the queue, guests see exposed rebar and crumbling concrete walls covered in moss. They walk inside the building and into a "ritual cave," which features cave paintings of native Na'vi warriors and their banshees. There follows an underground bunker, with steel doors and concrete walls. Once through that section of the queue, guests walk past an area where foliage and rocks glow brightly. A sign near the rockwork identifies this area as the Mountain Banshee Project.

From here, guests enter a laboratory, similar in design to the lab occupied by Dr. Grace Augustine in *Avatar*, where they witness several experiments. There's also a piece of unobtanium (the object of the RDA's fanatical quest) on display. Easily the most eye-catching element of this section of the queue is a 12-foot long blue Na'vi avatar encased in a giant tube filled with bubbling liquid. Guests on the FastPass queue miss out on this part of the attraction.

In the next part of the queue, guests are "scanned" to find an avatar that they are best matched with genetically.

Finally, it's time to board your banshee. You'll take a seat in what is called a "link chair," which resembles a small motorcycle. There are handles in front and once you've put on your 3-D glasses, three restraints (one at your back and two at your calves) gently lock you in place. After a few anxious seconds, the wall in front of you opens and you find yourself high atop a Pandoran cliff. Your banshee, unsteady and seemingly unafraid, jumps off the cliff and takes flight. You fly dangerously close to tree limbs and the legendary Pandoran floating mountains...up and down in random fashion, until you approach an ocean, where you swoop under a giant wave created by a breaching, whale-like creature.

All the while, you can feel your banshee breathing underneath you, hear its wings flap and smell musty aromas. After a stop in a bioluminescent cave, your banshee takes off again, more confident and steady, through more of Pandora's natural wonders before your flight comes to an end.

Perhaps the most amazing aspect of the experience is the fact that your link chair never moves from its fixed position. But the sensation of flight is quite real and the overall sensation of exhilaration stays with guests long after the flight has ended.

It's Tough to Be a Bug!

It doesn't matter how cute you are,
Or even if you're practically rare.
When most people spot you,
They're upset to see you there.

They squish you, and swat you
Or scream and run for the spray.

Without even realizing all the good,
Your labor has brought their way.

Before you doom every bug,
Take time to discover what they do.

The mission of most insects,
Is simply to ensure a healthier you.

IT REALLY IS TOUGH TO BE A BUG

The It's Tough to Be a Bug! 3-D attraction, located inside the base the Tree of Life in Animal Kingdom and in Disney California Adventure, celebrates the misunderstood world of insects. It's a classic example of Disney's penchant for "edu-tainment": educating you while serving up some great entertainment.

There were several ideas on the table for the base of the Tree of Life when it was in the planning stages. One was for a dining space, tentatively to be called the Roots Restaurant.

Imagineer Kevin Rafferty was in a meeting with Disney CEO Michael Eisner when the boss ditched the restaurant idea and asked if a show could be placed inside the tree's massive root system. "Yeah, we could probably put a couple hundred seats in that thing," was Rafferty's response. He was then given the task of coming up with a show for the new venue.

Rafferty's first inclination was to tap into the success of Disney's animated classic *The Lion King*. "I came up with a show that had Rafiki, the wise old sage from *The Lion King*, talking about the animal kingdom."

Eisner thought it was a great idea—but not great enough.

He suggested that Rafferty turn to the world of insects for inspiration and that he should consult with the folks at Pixar Animation, who were in the middle of creating their latest movie, *A Bug's Life*. At first, Rafferty didn't see the correlation between bugs and animals, but during his research, he learned just how important insects are to both man and the animal kingdom.

Insects pollinate plants, allowing them to reproduce, and they have a voracious appetite for waste. "Without bugs, we'd be in a world of hurt," Rafferty concluded.

It's Tough to Be a Bug! evolved into a show which told the story of man's misguided quest to eliminate bugs from the face of the Earth—which, if successful, would prove to be catastrophic. It used 1950s-era film clips to further show man's warped perception of insects, as well as introducing new characters who make their presence felt in a variety of interesting ways, like a soldier termite that sprays "acid" on the audience, or a Chilean tarantula who doles out poisonous quills.

The stars of the show are Audio-Animatronics figures of Flik and Hopper, both stars of *A Bug's Life*. A variety of in-theater special effects and gags enhance the production, including the always alarming stink bug effect, as well as the "butt bug" effect, where guests feel "bugs" crawling under their seats.

The pre-show queue area features a variety of Broadway-style posters which inform guests of previous shows that have been staged in the theater, things like "A Cockroach Line" and "Beauty and the Bees."

CHAPTER FIVE

Disney Springs

Disney Springs Springs to Life

If saving money has become your mission,
Disney Springs doesn't charge admission.

Bring your family or your favorite sweetie,
To discover a free space created by Mickey.

There are more dining options than you'd think,
The Springs offers over 50 places to eat or drink.

Numerous little shops have their very own themes,
Allowing you to buy the souvenirs of your dreams.

Take the ferry, park your car, or ride the bus
Disney Springs is most certainly a must.

Just Like Home

Most anything you can do at home,
You can do within Disney Springs.

Watch a first-run movie, go bowling,
Or shop for elegant clothes or wedding rings.

You can sit dockside while margarita drinking,
Or go to a pub for dinner and view step-dancing.

There's more in common with your hometown,
Than you could ever manage to be thinking.

Disney Springs Guest Services

Rent a stroller or wheelchair if you left yours at home,
Ask to locate your lost parents if suddenly you're all alone.

Obtain a map to see where you are and where you want to be,
Ask highlights and directions to all the places you want to see.
Guest Services can tell where to find first aid, gas, or an ATM,
Your vacation will go smoother with a little help from them.

The LEGO Store

My grandkids love to play at the LEGO store,
Putting contraptions together for an hour or more.

As the years go by our family playtime increases,
So we purchase additional LEGOs in boxes and in pieces.

Buying those small plastic bricks, mostly yellow, red, and blue,
Always keeps our grandkids busy in our hotel room, too.

We can spend our day in a not-too-expensive way,
And give the kids mementos of their magical vacation stay.

THE EVOLUTION OF DISNEY'S SHOPPING / DINING/ENTERTAINMENT DISTRICT

When it comes to name changes, Disney Springs is the unquestioned leader on Walt Disney World property.

In 1975, WDW introduced the Lake Buena Vista Shopping Village, a quaint area which gave Disney guests the option of shopping in a leisurely setting, away from the hustle-and-bustle of the Magic Kingdom. "The Village," as it became known, was a small, yet ambitious project. There were small stores and eateries at the northern end of Lake Buena Vista (roughly where the Rainforest Café and the World of Disney are located today). The *Empress Lilly*, a restaurant that looked like a riverboat and did, in fact, sit in the water, anchored the lake-side area.

In 1977, the area was renamed the Walt Disney World Village, better tying it in to the Walt Disney World theme. By the time 1989 rolled around, Walt Disney World now featured Epcot and the Disney-MGM Studios theme parks, so with guests on property, the Walt Disney World Village was expanded and renamed again, this time to the Disney Village Marketplace. In addition, a new adult entertainment district, Pleasure Island, was added to the mix, along with trendy restaurants and nightclubs.

In 1997, the complex was reimagined yet again and became known as Downtown Disney, divided into the East Side and the West Side. New entertainment and dining options included a Cirque du Soleil theater, DisneyQuest, a Virgin megastore, the conversion of the Mickey's Character Shop into the massive World of Disney, and the opening of a Rainforest Café and a Planet Hollywood.

In 2013, a few years after Pleasure Island was closed, Disney began its most ambitious expansion of the area to date and Disney Springs was born. Disney Springs is divided into four distinct "neighborhoods": the Marketplace, the Landing, Town Center, and West Side. Each area features its own architectural style and, typical of Disney's creativity, is awash in detail and exquisite design elements.

As part of the work, Buena Vista Drive was expanded with an eye toward improving traffic flow (there are now three lanes of traffic in either direction, with two dedicated bus lanes in the center of the roadway). Most of the original parking lots were re-purposed and replaced by two multi-level parking garages and a wide assortment of high-end retailers, interesting niche shops, and enough eateries to satisfy any and all taste buds.

Also added to the complex were two pedestrian bridges, one leading from the Marketplace to the Landing, the other allowing guests easy access to Disney's Saratoga Springs Resort. Boat service in small pontoon watercraft was expanded. In addition to boats carrying guests from the Old Key West, Port Orleans, and Saratoga Springs resorts, there are boats shuttling guests from one end of Disney Springs to the other. And a large outdoor bus station is now located in the center of the property.

The 'Empress Lilly'

If breakfast has ever been fun for you,
The Empress Lilly *should have been a must for you.*

It was a place where Pluto would share a morning cup of tea,
Or you could chat with Tweedle Dum and Tweedle Dee.

Robin Hood, Donald Duck, or Goofy might have stopped by,
To spend time having breakfast with you and I.

Mickey Mouse, fruit salad, and freshly made muffins, too,
How could mornings ever be more fun for you?

SAILING THROUGH THE YEARS
ON THE 'EMPRESS LILLY'

The *Empress Lilly*, named after Walt Disney's wife Lillian Bounds Disney, was christened on May 1, 1976, by Lillian Disney herself, although the replica Mississippi River paddle wheeler was, in reality, a boat-shaped building that rested on a concrete foundation embedded in the waters of Lake Buena Vista off what was then known as the Disney Village Marketplace.

The 220-foot-long *Empress Lilly* was a faux floating dining and entertainment facility, featuring three unique, dinner-only restaurants (Fisherman's Deck, Steerman's Quarters, and the Empress Room) and a jazz lounge (Baton Rouge Lounge). The *Empress Lilly* was one of the first on-property locations to feature character breakfasts, known then as Breakfast a la Disney.

Walt Disney Imagineering was responsible for the classic riverboat design of the *Empress Lilly*, which featured gingerbread scrollwork, stained glass, and two tall smokestacks among its many intricate details. To add to its authentic characteristics, the paddle wheel to the aft of the boat churned constantly.

During the mid-1990s, Disney opted to have outside concerns take over some of its on-property restaurants. Rights to operate the *Empress Lilly* were sold to Levy

Restaurants, which signed a 20-year contract and over-hauled the ship. Both the interior and exterior were renovated, with a new décor featuring a single restaurant. The old, rusting smokestacks and paddle wheel were removed. The *Empress Lilly* was closed on April 22, 1995, and reopened as Fulton's Crab House on March 10, 1996.

In 2016, Fulton's Crab House closed for another make-over, in part to reflect the expansion and rebranding of the shopping and entertainment district now known as Disney Springs, and in part for another major interior and exterior renovation. The restaurant, renamed Paddlefish, is an eclectic, seafood-centric facility that offers multiple dining experiences and private event spaces; it's still operated by Levy Restaurants.

To the delight of purists, the paddle wheel and smoke-stacks were re-installed during the recent renovation, giving the stylishly modern décor a nostalgic feel.

A Balloon Ride Like No Other

Riding above the trees in a hot-air balloon,
I'm so close to the stars I can touch the moon.
Rapidly ascending higher toward the sky,
I hear the wind softly whisper a sweet lullaby.
Nowhere could ever be as tranquil as soaring up above,
Observing the Earth below me like a peaceful dove.

A BIRD'S-EYE VIEW OF WALT DISNEY WORLD

In 2005, Walt Disney World "borrowed" several attractions that were popular at other Disney parks around the world.

Soarin' Over California, a mainstay at Disney California Adventure, took up residence in The Land pavilion at Epcot. A princess castle show, popular at Tokyo Disneyland, was staged at the Magic Kingdom in WDW. Lights, Motors, Action!...Extreme Stunt Show, a big hit in Disneyland Paris, came to Disney's Hollywood Studios.

And Characters in Flight, a popular diversion at Downtown Disney in Disneyland Paris, took up residence in Florida at what is now known as Disney Springs.

The tethered helium balloon experience was custom-built for Disney by a company based in Paris, France, called Aerophile S.A. The boarding area for Characters in Flight is located in the Landing neighborhood of Disney Springs.

The balloon itself was originally designed and constructed to feature the silhouettes of some of Disney's most recognizable characters who are associated with flight. A recent re-imagining of the balloon features a fresh design inspired by the springs and the element of water.

Since the balloon is tethered to the ground, it won't rise higher than 400 feet at any time. As you might expect with an outdoor attraction, Characters in Flight is subject to the vagaries of weather. The attraction is grounded if winds exceed 28 mph in the air, 18 mph on the ground, or if there is a storm or lightning in the area.

Guests aboard Characters in Flight get a breathtaking 360-degree view of Walt Disney World for approximately 8–10 minutes. The daily hours of operation are 8:30 a.m. to midnight, weather permitting.

Pizza at the Springs

Pizza has become my all-time favorite passion,
I love my pizza served any way, type, or fashion.
Deep dish, thin or thick crust, square or round,
At Disney Springs, all types of pizza can be found.
But Pizza Ponte is the best place to take your bambino,
Because the Italian food there is always "cosi buono."

Rainforest Café

Have you ever visited a Rainforest Café,
And sampled the safari soup of the day?

Zucchini, tomatoes, pasta, and cheese,
It's a hearty item that's sure to please.
Carnivorous or vegan, you'll find what you like,
It's a tropical-like location to spend your night.

Raglan Road

Enjoy a Cookes Tour by sampling Irish fare,
And raising a pint or two while you're there.
You'll be entertained by beautiful Irish lasses,
Singing traditional ballads and Celtic dances.
It's heard the pub was moved here brick by brick,
If you choose to make reservations, do it quick.
Raglan Road serves authentic fish and chips,
And a menu including your favorite dish.
One of the finest places in Disney Springs,
A fine place to dine or purchase Irish things.

FOOD OPTIONS WITHIN DISNEY SPRINGS ARE MANY AND VARIED

Disney Springs, one of the premier shopping/dining/entertainment venues in all of Florida, boasts food options that appeal to every taste bud, no matter how discerning.

From salads to sushi, burgers to beef stew, fried chicken to fish and chips, you'll find it at Disney Springs, which boasts an unrivaled lineup of quality restaurants, most created by some of the world's most prominent chefs. For those who want to keep it simple and less flashy, there's an area in the Exposition Park section of Disney Springs' West Side neighborhood where food trucks hold sway.

Regarding the three eateries featured in the introductory poem:

Pizza Ponte, located in the Landing, prides itself on quick, yet high-quality Italian offerings.

Raglan Road Irish Pub and Restaurant, also located in the Landing, is as much about the spirited Irish entertainment as it is about the authentic Irish cuisine. You can satisfy a yearning for fresh and fast Irish fare at Cookes of Dublin, a counter-service establishment located beside Raglan Road. You'll find a variety of Dublin-style dishes like fish and chips, meat pies, and grilled wild boar burgers. Inside Raglan Road, there's an expanded menu of traditional Irish dishes that pair perfectly with the lively entertainment and libations that would make St. Patrick proud.

And Rainforest Café, the self-proclaimed wild place to shop and eat, offers a different restaurant experience, where the sights and sounds of a typical rainforest play out regularly as you dine. The exterior of the venue, which is shaped like a volcano, erupts on cue every few minutes, with flames shooting out into the sky.

The remaining food options within Disney Springs' confines represent an eclectic mix of some of the world's most distinctive cuisine.

Bongo's Cuban Café, House of Blues, Paradiso 37, Planet Hollywood, and T-REX have been featured for several years.

The Boathouse, Chef Art Smith's Homecoming, the Edison, Maria & Enzo's Frontera Cocina, Morimoto Asia, Terralina Crafted Italian, Splitsville Dining Room, and STK Orlando have been introduced to the Disney Springs menu over the last few years. Paddlefish, located in the waters of Lake Buena Vista, is the re-imagined version of the former *Empress Lilly*.

Many of these establishments also offer quick-service food and beverages. Other quick-service options in Disney Springs include D-Luxe Burger, Earl of Sandwich, Polite Pig, and Ghirardelli's Ice Cream.

In addition, there are a host of carts and kiosks scattered around Disney Springs, offering candy, pretzels, ice cream, coffee and beverages, Italian ice, and hand-crafted smoothies.

CHAPTER SIX

Disney Resorts

Disney Resort Hotels

Disney has twenty-five on-site hotels to choose from;
To ensure a perfect stay, use this handy rule of thumb.

There's value, moderate, deluxe, and villa-style accommodations,
Know what you prefer before you make your reservations.

Affordable value hotels are great if you have kids in tow,
But honeymooners may prefer a luxurious secluded bungalow.

Staying on-site can come with many magical advantages,
As well as an assortment of varied discounted packages.

Most hotels often offer unlimited time on your wireless devices,
Advance FastPasses and extra hours at the parks are priceless.

Old Key West

Old Key West is Florida the way it should be,
So much to do for your entire family.

Surrounded by old-time treats and gourmet delights,
Bringing your appetite to new magical heights.

Sit by the pool or take a leisurely ride on the ferry,
No matter when you visit, your vacation will be merry.

STAYING WHERE THE MAGIC IS

During the late 1980s, Disney took stock of its on-property resorts at Walt Disney World and drew a sobering conclusion: too many guests were staying off-property, spending much of their time—and money—away from Disney.

According to the late Charlie Ridgway, former chief of Walt Disney World press and publicity: "If there was one thing lacking on our part [at that time], it was in the fact that we didn't keep up with on-site hotel accommodations." Keeping Disney guests on Disney property during the length of their stay became a priority.

Thus began a concerted effort on Disney's part to build more resorts on Walt Disney World's 27,000-plus acre property. New resorts, each with a specific theme, began springing up. During this ambitious time of growth and expansion, Disney also came up with a concept that would revolutionize the way guests visited Walt Disney World: time sharing, but with an important twist. Guests could purchase a real estate interest in Disney—an actual piece of the magic. This new vacation concept was called the Disney Vacation Club, or DVC for short.

The very first DVC property, known initially as the Disney Vacation Club Resort, opened on December 20, 1991. It was renamed the Old Key West Resort in 1996, after Disney's Vero Beach Resort opened in 1995 and just prior to the opening of Disney's Hilton Head Resort in South Carolina.

Unlike other time-share programs at the time, which locked its members into specific times of the year, DVC uses an innovative points system, which gives owners the flexibility of coming to Disney any time of the year they'd like—pending availability, of course. In addition, DVC owners can borrow or bank their points, or even purchase more points as their needs change. Points are renewed every 12 months and owners are responsible for paying yearly dues.

The DVC concept took off beyond anyone's wildest dreams and Disney began expanding its profile by building Vacation Club additions to existing resorts at Walt Disney World. There are now DVC properties near the Magic Kingdom at the Contemporary (Bay Lake Tower),

Polynesian (villas and bungalows), and Grand Floridian and Wilderness Lodge resorts (Copper Creek and Boulder Creek). A short distance from Epcot, DVC has a presence at the BoardWalk and Beach Club resorts. Across Lake Buena Vista and Disney Springs sits Saratoga Springs, the largest DVC property at Walt Disney World. And adjacent to Disney's Animal Kingdom park, there's Kidani Village. Nearby Jambo House has several DVC-dedicated rooms, as well as a concierge level for members.

At Disneyland, there are DVC-dedicated rooms in the Grand Californian, and in perhaps its most ambitious project to date, DVC opened a lavish seaside resort in Ko Olina, Oahu, Hawaii, called Aulani.

The Contemporary Resort

Walk through one of Disney's finest resorts at your freedom,
Chief Mickey's has one of the best buffets in the kingdom.

Dine in the California Grill to see fireworks in the sky,
Listen to the hum of the monorail while it quickly passes by.

Choose from a multitude of assorted types of recreation
The Contemporary is a fabulous choice for your next vacation.

DISNEY'S CONTEMPORARY RESORT WAS DESIGNED TO BE 'LIKE A CHEST OF DRAWERS'

Even though Disney's Contemporary Resort evokes a modern, futuristic style, itl has a long, storied history.

The Contemporary was one of five themed hotels planned for the area rimming Seven Seas Lagoon near the Magic Kingdom when Walt Disney World was in the design phase in the late 1960s. Only two of those resorts—the Contemporary and the Polynesian—made it past the drawing board and opened along with the Magic Kingdom in October of 1971.

In designing the two hotels, Disney and U.S. Steel opted to employ new building techniques. "We actually built the rooms off-site," said former Imagineering executive Marty Sklar. "Everything was bolted down—all the fixtures, furniture, and appliances. Then we trucked each room to the building site, where the frame was already in place. The rooms were then inserted into the frame, like a chest of drawers."

The thinking was, when the rooms needed to be updated, they could simply be removed and then replaced by newer versions. There was one problem: the designers didn't take into account that the buildings would "settle," making it impossible for the rooms to be removed as planned.

Despite that hiccup, the Contemporary remains one of the most striking and iconic hotels on Walt Disney World property. For one thing, its distinctive A-frame design is eye-catching. For another, the Walt Disney World monorail runs right through the hotel's Grand Canyon Concourse, making for some stunning photos and, to this day, leaving most first-time guests with a look of wide-eyed wonder as the monorail quietly glides through.

The most prominent feature in the Contemporary's fourth-floor main concourse is a massive tile mural designed by artist Mary Blair, which covers the hotel's main elevator shaft. Her 184-feet-tall masterpiece consists of 1,800 one-foot-square tiles that depict Native American children in Blair's bold, colorful, and rounded style. It took 18 months to complete. Blair and the other artists who toiled on the project autographed several tiles located at the base of the work.

The concourse is home to Chef Mickey's character meals, as well as the Contempo Café, serving classic American dishes. The Wave, serving mostly healthy American food, is located on the ground floor adjacent to the check-in area. There's also the California Grill, located on the 15th floor, which offers fine dining options as well as spectacular views of the surrounding areas and the fireworks displays ignited in and around the Magic Kingdom.

The Contemporary has a smaller adjoining section, known as the South Tower wing. When the hotel opened, there also was a North Tower wing, but that was torn down to make room for Bay Lake Tower, a Disney Vacation Club resort. The Contemporary and Bay Lake Tower are linked by a bridge walkway.

The Contemporary also is home to one of the largest convention centers on Disney property. It was inside this site on Nov. 17, 1973, where President Richard Nixon gave his infamous "I am not a crook" speech in front of a gathering of Associated Press managing editors.

Guests can either walk, take a monorail, or hop on one of the many watercraft that ply the waters of Bay Lake and Seven Seas Lagoon to reach the Magic Kingdom. Guests may also board a monorail at the Transportation & Ticket Center to get to Epcot. One of the largest bus depots on WDW property is located across the street from the Contemporary.

One little-known fact about the Contemporary: when it came time to name the futuristic resort, several choices were bandied about. Marty Sklar didn't quite care for Contemporary. "That's not a name, it's a description," he said. He prepared a detailed presentation for Disney CEO Roy O. Disney, pushing hard for his own personal favorite name, Tempo Bay. After hearing Sklar out, Roy Disney turned to him and said: "What's wrong with Contemporary?"

More than 40 years later, Sklar responded: "What *is* wrong with Contemporary? It's a great name!"

Port Orleans French Quarter

You're always a special guest at Port Orleans,
Whether you are ninety-nine or in your teens.
Every day is Mardi Gras, every day is fun,
It's always wonderful in the rain or in the sun.

Take a ferry downtown or ride on a serpent water slide,
Then listen to smooth jazz when you go back inside.
Spending time at the Port Orleans French Quarter,
Is always great, regardless if you're ashore or in the water.

HOW'S BAYOU?

New Orleans was one of Walt Disney's favorite cities. In fact, during one memorable visit in the mid-1960s, he took members of his family and a few of his company's key designers and developers to New Orleans on a fact-finding tour of the city. Their mission was to research the Crescent City, immersing themselves in its people and culture in advance of creating New Orleans Square in Disneyland.

The Port Orleans resorts at Walt Disney World offers guests a slice of New Orleans and NOLA's surrounding waterways and bayous.

The resort is divided into two sections: French Quarter and Riverside. The entire complex surrounds a body of water known as the Sassagoula River that connects Port Orleans to Disney Springs. Guests can board boats for the journey back and forth.

Port Orleans French Quarter and Riverside are awash in authentic details of Louisiana's most fabled city. New Orleans' rich heritage and distinctive themes permeate the Port Orleans property. There are intricate wrought-iron railings, cobblestone streets, gas lamps, and courtyards filled with blooming flowers that capture the spirit and romance of New Orleans' French Quarter. Many of the buildings on property reflect the antebellum style common in the South prior to the Civil War.

Port Orleans French Quarter boasts one of the most unique pools in all of Walt Disney World, where King Neptune presides over the fun and youngsters careen down a giant slide in the shape of a sea serpent.

The River Roost Lounge is a popular nightspot for guests, with live jazz entertainment. The French Quarter offers a children's pool, whirlpool spa, playground, arcade, jogging trail, bike rentals, carriage rides, a gift shop, and laundry facilities.

Much like the French Quarter, Port Orleans Riverside evokes the casual charm of a bygone era, complete with the rustic beauty and gracious hospitality of the bayou. Riverside features Disney character-themed rooms, a chartered Pirate Adventure Cruise, and a swimmin' hole hideaway.

Kona Café, 'Ohana, and the Polynesian

I have my preferred places at every Disney resort,
And the Polynesian has my favorite restaurant of sort.
The Kona Café creates the most delicious meals,
Their Tonga toast has me feeling head over heels.

Magical deep-fried French toast stuffed with bananas,
Another Polynesian restaurant I love is 'Ohana.
A breakfast buffet with so many different choices,
Whenever we go there, my family rejoices.

A SLICE OF SOUTH SEAS LIFE AT DISNEY'S POLYNESIAN VILLAGE RESORT

Like the Contemporary, Disney's Polynesian Village opened on Oct. 1, 1971, along with the Magic Kingdom. The Polynesian is a AAA Four-Diamond award-winning resort located on the shores of the Seven Seas Lagoon across from the Magic Kingdom. Much like the Contemporary, its rooms were built off-site; unlike the Contemporary, where the rooms were inserted into a steel form, the Polynesian's rooms were stacked, with the framework and concrete placed around them.

The Polynesian is located within walking distance of the Transportation & Ticket Center where guests can catch a ferry boat to the Magic Kingdom, or a monorail to

Magic Kingdom or Epcot. The Polynesian hotel is located on the monorail resort loop (along with the Grand Floridian and the Contemporary) and offers water launch transportation.

The focal point of the Polynesian is the Great Ceremonial House, designed after a royal assembly lodge in Tahiti. It houses the resort's guest services area and main lobby. The Great Ceremonial House also contains most of the resort's shopping and dining options. For 33 years, the Great Ceremonial House was known for its large tropical waterfall centerpiece, which included more than 75 species of plant life. The display was removed in 2014 and was replaced by a more traditional atrium.

The property features 11 two- and three-story longhouses, each named for an island in Polynesia: Tonga, Fiji, Niue, Samoa, Rarotonga, Tahiti, Tokelau, Rapa Nui, Tuvalu, Aotearoa and Hawaii. Between 2013 and 2015, 20 bungalows built on stilts over the Seven Seas Lagoon were added. The new area, known as Bora Bora, is open to Disney Vacation Club members.

Disney's Polynesian Village Resort has 847 rooms spread out over 39 acres. It is styled as a South Pacific paradise, complete with a pool (Nanea) that features a volcano-like structure with a built-in water slide, tropical landscaping with swaying palm trees, waterfalls, and bamboo Tiki torches.

Dining options include Kona Café, which offers table service and a South Pacific-inspired menu, and 'Ohana, with its all-you-care-to-eat character breakfast and dinner meals. There's also Trader Sam's Grog Grotto, an interactive bar and lounge.

The Polynesian also is home to the Spirit of Aloha Dinner Show, presented every Tuesday through Saturday (weather permitting) at Luau Cove. Both the entertainment and the food are typical of what you might experience during a traditional Polynesian luau.

The main gift shop at the Polynesian, BouTIKI, specializes in souvenirs and men's and women's fashions. Trader Jack's and Samoa Snacks, as well as a Wyland Gallery, round out the retail options.

There's one historical tidbit about the Polynesian Resort worth sharing: on Dec. 29, 1974, a hotel guest by the name of John Lennon signed the legal papers to officially dissolve the Beatles, the band he co-founded in the late 1950s.

On the Corner of BoardWalk and Happiness

Sitting on my balcony watching entertainers below,
I almost felt like a child watching a circus show.

Jugglers, musicians, and vendors of every kind,
A vaudeville show was quickly brought to mind.

The BoardWalk hotel is definitely like no other,
And the Atlantic Dance Hall usually has no cover.

BoardWalk balcony rooms give you so much to see,
It's like visiting a 1920s day in Atlantic City.

ATLANTIC CITY'S GLORY DAYS ARE REPLICATED AT THE BOARDWALK

Disney's BoardWalk Inn is more than just a hotel and entertainment complex. It's a walk down memory lane.

Those who remember the glory days of the East Coast's grand seaside resorts—and in particular, Atlantic City in New Jersey and Coney Island in Brooklyn, New York—will have their memories pleasantly jogged during a visit to Disney's BoardWalk Inn & Villas. The massive complex, located on the shores of Crescent Lake, opened in 1996 and sits within view of Disney's Yacht and Beach Club resorts and the Swan and Dolphin hotels. The BoardWalk also is centrally located between Epcot and Hollywood Studios. The resort, as well as other features surrounding it, were designed by Robert A.M. Stern Architects.

In keeping with its coastal theming, the BoardWalk is surrounded by a ¼-mile-long wooden-planked board-walk. Guests can rent surreys or bicycles to navigate the boardwalk or they can take a relaxing stroll and watch as numerous watercraft ply the nearby lake. Along the way, they can stop to partake of classic midway games or be entertained by street performers.

There also are numerous shopping and dining options available as guests stroll along the boardwalk, including Big River Grille & Brewing Works (the only micro-brewery on Walt Disney World property), the Boardwalk Bakery, Trattorina al Forno Italian restaurant, an ESPN Club, the Flying Fish Café, and Ample Hills Creamery. In addition, there are two nightclubs—the Atlantic Dance Hall and Jellyrolls, known for its dueling pianos—which keep the entertainment flowing into the wee hours.

There are shopping options available as well, with Dundry's Sundries, the Screen Door General Store, and Wyland Galleries topping the list.

Both the BoardWalk Inn, a AAA Four-Diamond award-winning hotel, and the BoardWalk Villas share a common lobby. The inn's décor was inspired by the resorts located up and down the eastern seaboard in the 20th century. The villas, meanwhile, are part of the Disney Vacation Club and feature larger multi-bedroom suites.

The property features three themed pools. The feature pool, Luna Park, is themed after a carnival, circa 1930s. Luna Park includes the distinctive 200-foot Keister Coaster water slide. Also in the Luna Park area is the Luna Park Crazy House, a play area for young children.

The BoardWalk's location allows guests to walk to either Epcot or Hollywood Studios (it's about a mile walk to Hollywood Studios' main entrance, along trails that hug water canals, and a shorter walk to Epcot's World Showcase entryway). There's also boat service available to the two parks or to the neighboring resorts along Crescent Lake.

Victoria and Albert's

I loved the Mickey Mouse Club when I was eight,
And I adored my Mickey cup and my Mickey plate.
But now I realize English china is simply divine,
And I love dinning with my prince at dinner time.
Elegant and posh, sipping a splash of champagne,
Victoria and Albert's is quite far from mundane.

ELEGANT DINING IN THE HEART OF WALT DISNEY WORLD

Of all the dining options available on Walt Disney World property, Victoria & Albert's in the Grand Floridian Resort and Spa is considered the crème de la crème.

To give you an idea of just how well-respected Victoria & Albert's is, it has received the prestigious AAA Five-Diamond rating for 17 consecutive years. There are just 47 AAA Five-Diamond restaurants in the United States, with only three in Florida. Victoria & Albert's also has received the Forbes Travel Guide four-star rating and glowing reviews from Zagat.

Like the Grand Floridian itself, Victoria and Albert's is a throwback to the days of elegance, when fine dining meant meals were served in courses and well-dressed diners were expected to savor every last detail of their dining experience. Fine china and crystal? But of course.

Victoria & Albert's features modern American cuisine with exquisite products sourced from around the world—truffles from Italy, fresh herbs from Ohio, beef from Japan, poulet rouge from North Carolina, oysters from North Florida, and the finest caviar.

Executive Chef Scott Hunnel has assembled a talented and experienced staff: chef de cuisine Aimee Rivera, master pastry chef Erich Herbitschek, and maitre d'hotel Israel Perez, all of whom wear classic white toques. The talented culinary team's long-standing approach shows imagination, and the food is treated as an art form, featuring aromatic flavors, vivid colors, exciting textures, and exquisite wine pairings with each course.

Each season has its own flavors and colors, and each day the kitchen selects whatever is fresh at the market to create menus for the Dining Room, Queen Victoria's Room, and the Chef's Table. With a wealth of resources from farmers, fishermen, and artisans, the kitchen sources pristine ingredients for such dishes as the Spanish octopus with Iberico ham and sherry vinaigrette and poached local chicken egg with Florida corn and crayfish.

Saratoga Springs

Sitting near the pool at Saratoga Springs,
Thinking of the blessings that life sometimes brings.

Listening to children laugh as they play on the slide,
As I wave from my lounge chair on the nice shady side.

This evening I'll watch fireworks from our balcony,
With my grandsons giggling with amazement and glee.

SARATOGA SPRINGS STARTED OUT AS AN ARTISTS' COLONY

At the dawn of the 1990s, Disney CEO Michael Eisner declared that the next 10 years would be known as "the Disney Decade."

During the 1990s, plans were set in motion to expand the Disney profile: more park attractions, more theme parks, more resort options, and even an entry into the cruise ship industry.

One of the Eisner-inspired projects was the creation of the Disney Institute, which opened in 1996 with a large campus across from what was then the Downtown Disney shopping district, now known as Disney Springs. Eisner envisioned the Disney Institute as a new way to vacation, an artists' colony that put an emphasis on learning and interactive experiences. Guests were offered programs in cooking, floral arranging, outdoor adventures (such as rock climbing or golf lessons), animation, photography, and TV production.

Guests were housed on the Disney Institute campus, which also included a conference center, 28 program studios, a performance center, outdoor amphitheater, a movie theater, a sports and fitness center, and a radio and closed-circuit TV stations.

To Eisner's chagrin, the idea never caught on as guests just didn't want to "get educated" during their vacations. The Disney Institute's campus was closed in 2003 and plans were set in motion to expand the property and transform it into a Disney Vacation Club resort.

The new resort, renamed Saratoga Springs, was inspired by the city of Saratoga Springs in upstate New York. It has a quaint Victorian feel, reminiscent of Saratoga Springs, circa 1880, when the area was among the top tourist attractions in the country.

Saratoga Springs has a horse racing theme, reflected in many of its design elements. It was opened in phases, beginning in 2004. When construction and renovations were completed, Saratoga Springs became the largest DVC resort on Walt Disney World property. It has two main dining options: Artist's Palette and the Turf Club Bar and Grill. There also are five pools spread out on the campus. The resort is home to the Lake Buena Vista Golf Course, which has hosted PGA, LPGA, and USGA events.

The Saratoga Springs campus, located across Lake Buena Vista from Disney Springs, is divided into five sections: the Springs, the Carousel, the Paddock, Congress Park, and the Grandstand. Many of the original Disney Institute structures were repurposed to accommodate DVC. The movie theater and the sports and fitness center, for example, are now where the DVC's offices and promotional facilities are based.

While the Disney Institute campus was re-imagined, the concept of the institute has morphed into a professional development wing of the Walt Disney Company, showcasing all of the business aspects behind the Disney magic. Disney Institute conducts seminars, workshops, and presentations geared to enriching business professionals.

Bay Lake Tower

On a balcony looking over a sandy beach,
Snacking on a salad of cream cheese and peach.
Watching boats slowly crossing the bay,
Is the most beautiful part of my Disney day.
Surrounded by the sweet aroma of hibiscus,
I see honeymooners exchanging hugs and kisses.
Gentle waves glitter in the daytime sun,
Could vacation ever be more fun?

THE EVOLUTION OF BAY LAKE TOWER

When Walt Disney World was being developed in the late 1960s, a total of five resort hotels were on the drawing board, to be built along the shores of the artificial Seven Seas Lagoon or the existing Bay Lake, all within view of the Magic Kingdom. One would have a Polynesian theme, another would be contemporary in design, while the others would be Persian, Asian, and Venetian themed.

Only the Polynesian and Contemporary made it off the drawing board, with both opening in the fall of 1971.

In 1988, Disney's Grand Floridian Resort & Spa was added to the Seven Seas Lagoon lineup. The Grand Floridian is an homage to the Victorian-era hotels of Florida's east coast in the 19th century and was modeled after the Mount Washington Resort in New Hampshire and the Hotel del Coronado in California.

In 2009, Bay Lake Tower, a Disney Vacation Club resort, debuted alongside the Contemporary, putting DVC members within walking distance to the Magic Kingdom and giving them access to the monorail as well as all of the Contemporary's amenities.

Bay Lake Tower, designed by architect Charles Gwathmey, was built in the shape of a U, as opposed to the Contemporary's A-frame design. To make room for the new resort, the Contemporary's North Garden Wing and a tennis club had to be demolished. Because of its unique design, all of the 428 rooms in Bay Lake Tower are wedge shaped. Its rooms come in three categories: Magic Kingdom view, Bay Lake view, and standard view.

Bay Lake Tower shares the same modern feel as the Contemporary. The two buildings are linked by a winding sky bridge, allowing Bay Lake Tower guests complete access to the Contemporary's restaurants, gift shops, the monorail station, and a boat system that links with the Magic Kingdom and the nearby Wilderness Lodge.

Much like the Contemporary, which features the California Grill on its top floor, Bay Lake Tower is topped off by a lounge area called Top of the World (which, coincidentally, was the original name of the California Grill). Open to DVC guests, there's an indoor seating area with a full bar and limited food options. Outside the lounge is a viewing deck where guests get spectacular views of the Magic Kingdom and surrounding areas. The deck also offers a prime area to watch the nightly fireworks displays at the Magic Kingdom.

Jambo House View

If you've ever wished to take an African safari,
The Animal Kingdom Jambo House is a must.

Watch from your balcony as wild animals,
And savannahs are both so close to your touch.

Take photographs of everything that you see;
If you love animals, it's the best place to be.

S'mores at Disney's Animal Kingdom Lodge

The very best part of camping outdoors,
Is when nightfall comes we can all make s'mores.

Marshmallows carefully roasted over an open-fire pit,
Add chocolate and graham crackers and lickety split.

Warm and toasty goo that's simply sublime,
You've just created the best treat of all time.

GOOEY DELIGHTS AT JAMBO HOUSE AND KIDANI VILLAGE

At Animal Kingdom Lodge, be it at Jambo House or Kidani Village, there's an evening tradition (weather permitting) that delights young and old alike. Under careful cast member supervision, an open fire pit is ignited and guests are encouraged to take part in the time-honored tradition of roasting marshmallows. They receive long wooden sticks, place their marshmallows on the tip, and then dangle them into the roaring flames.

At Jambo House, marshmallow roasting is available at the Arusha Rock overlook area; at Kidani Village, the Savannah Overlook hosts the nightly experience.

Of course, guests are encouraged to stick around after they've enjoyed their sugary treats to watch the scores of animals who populate the resort's vast savannah as they get ready for the approaching nightfall. During this time, the animals are usually chowing down on their own version of gooey delights—mostly a vegetation called browse, which they consume in abundance.

In addition, a variety of cultural guides, from several different African nations, offer unique insights on the animals, as well as their homelands.

In its own special way, roasting marshmallows and observing the animals is Animal Kingdom Lodge's version of dinner and a show.

CHAPTER SEVEN

Mouselanious

The Best Time to Visit Disney

Go to Disney when most kids are in school,
Try to visit the when the hours are cool.
Early morning is usually the best,
Then return to your hotel to eat and rest.
I always stay somewhere at Disney on site,
So it's easier to return to the park at night.
Recharge your phone or pick up travel aids,
While your family is busy watching parades.
But no matter what time of the year or day,
Enjoy doing Disney your very own way.

WHEN IS THE BEST TIME TO VISIT DISNEY? ANY TIME YOU CAN.

When people find out that you're fond of all things Disney, they'll often ask you questions like, "What's so special about Disney?" or "Why do you always go *there* on vacation?" If your answers have piqued their interest, they might say something like, "Maybe we'll get there when our kids get a little older," followed by the inevitable: "When's the best time of the year to go?"

During the early days of both Disneyland and Walt Disney World, crowds and long lines for attractions were rarely an issue.

For many years after Disneyland opened, the park was closed on Mondays and Tuesdays. Crowds were heaviest on the weekends and during the summer as local residents and a few out-of-towners visited. At Walt Disney World, it took a few years before the Magic Kingdom hit its stride. According to the late Charlie Ridgway, former head of WDW press and publicity, "I can remember back in the early '70s, especially during the winter months, when we had maybe two or three thousand guests a day total."

Needless to say, things have changed over the years. Disneyland and Walt Disney World are open every day of the year, barring a catastrophic event. And attendance—and by extension, lines for attractions—is almost always booming. It's a rare day when the parks aren't crowded. When a new attraction is introduced, wait times can—and often do—exceed two-plus hours. Indeed, the addition of new attractions—or even entire new lands—makes the parks more enticing. So, too, is the growth and expansion of Disney's on-property resorts. As base-ball great Yogi Berra used to say: "People don't go there anymore; it's always crowded."

So, when is the best time to visit Disneyland or Walt Disney World? It depends.

For families with children in school, the window of opportunity is limited to times when the kids are off, which means the summer months, when the weather can be hot in southern California and downright oppressive in central Florida. Other times of the year when schools are off—like Christmas/New Year's, spring break, and Easter week—also tend to see large crowds swarming to Disney parks.

There was a time when the winter months were an optimal time to go to the parks, particularly because the weather is more comfortable. Older guests made this their go-to time to visit because of shorter lines, fewer crowds, green grass, and still-flowering foliage. But Disney seemed to notice that trend and starting packing in special events during those "off times" of the year in an effort to increase attendance—things like marathon weekends, cheerleading competitions, and seasonal festivals.

In an effort to optimize guests' visits to Disneyland and Walt Disney World, Disney has introduced initiatives that can make your day more enjoyable. For instance, Extra Magic Hours, where selected parks are open earlier or later to Disney resort guests, are one way to beat the crowds early in the day or late in the evening. So, too, is the use of the FastPass option, which allows guests to reserve a ride time in advance, then return to the attraction and get on the ride with little or no wait. And the single-rider line option allows guests to board selected attractions by themselves, often cutting wait times for that attraction by as much as half.

To most observers, however, there is no longer a "best time" to visit Disneyland or Walt Disney World. It all comes down to what time of year best fits with your plans.

A Vacation on the High Seas

We traveled from London to Oslo,
With a few stops in between.
Tea in Scotland, Aquavit in Iceland,
And nary the time to see the queen.
From the awesome cliffs of Dover,
To the beautiful streets of Stavanger.
From meeting familiar faces within the crew,
To departing a ship where no one is a stranger.
Watching the world from a balcony,
As we decide our next port adventures to do.
High mountain tops covered with ice and snow,
And crystal clear oceans of deep sapphire blue.
I love sailing on the Disney Cruise Line.
With so many places around the globe to roam.
My vacation was a truly magical one,
But it's so wonderful to be home.

Mickey Mouse on the Ocean Blue

I suppose there could be,
A much better place to be.

But I feel with all certainty,
Anywhere is best with a mouse named Mickey.

I love to sail with Mickey at sea,
You'll get a bracelet as your key.

Once you pay, most things are free,
There are extra charges certainly.

For some things that appeal to me,
My kids always like to water ski.

I always like taking a photo on safari,
There are always great shows for you to see.

A perfect holiday for you and me,
Is a vacation with Mickey at sea.

THE EVOLUTION OF THE DISNEY CRUISE LINE

The seeds for the Disney Cruise Line, which debuted in 1998 with the christening of the *Disney Magic*, were sown in 1985, when Disney partnered with Premier Cruises to offer what were known then as land-and-sea packages—guests would spend several days at Walt Disney World before heading over to Port Canaveral on the coast of the Atlantic Ocean and boarding one of Premier's Big Red Boats to enjoy a cruise through the Caribbean. It was billed as "America's No. 1 Family Cruise Vacation" and for several years, the association between Disney and Premier flourished. The Big Red Boats docked at Nassau in the Bahamas, staying in port long enough for guests to enjoy tours of the island, swimming and boating by day, as well as nightclub and gambling options during the evening.

During the course of the cruise, the Big Red Boats would make a stop at a private island in the Bahamas, where guests could take a tender from the ship and disembark onto a small dock. Guests visiting the island were told that what made it so special was the fact that it was used for some scenes for the TV show *Gilligan's Island*. In fact, many people went so far as to actually call the spit of land Gilligan's Island.

After a few years, the Disney hierarchy realized that the 10-year licensing agreement it had with Premier was troubling. For one thing, Premier's ships, built decades before the Americans with Disabilities Act, were not handicap accessible. For another, Disney was concerned that it didn't have complete control over what was being offered on the ships, mainly in the areas of guest service, cleanliness, food, and entertainment. And lastly, newer, much larger, and decidedly more upscale ocean liners were now plying the world's oceans, part of an industry-wide resurgence by all the major cruise lines, and would-be cruisers were flocking to these opulent "floating cities" and all they had to offer in droves.

Premier's Big Red Boats I, II, and III floundered after losing their Disney partnership in 1994. For a time, Premier hooked up with Universal, Walt Disney World's chief competitor for theme park guests in central Florida, in an effort to keep families with kids interested in cruising with them. Universal even offered characters from their own animation properties in an attempt to replicate what Disney had done.

But it wasn't to be. The end came swiftly for Premier. In one memorable week in September 2000, U.S. marshals seized all seven Premier cruise ships around the world, including the Big Red Boat II, which ended up being escorted to the Stapleton Navy home port on the New York City borough of Staten Island after being seized by marshals, having unloaded its unsuspecting passengers in Manhattan. It turns out the Big Red Boats, as well as their sister ships, were drowning in a sea of red ink. At the time, a recorded message on Premier's phone line said: "We regret to inform you that Premier Cruise Lines was forced to suspend operations of all our vessels indefinitely. Our lender has taken possession of the ships pursuant to the ships' mortgages." (In an ironic twist, the rusting hulk of the Big Red Boat II was seen docked in Nassau in the Bahamas during a port call by the *Disney Wonder* in January of 2002. The ship still had a distinctive, if fading, "P" on its funnel.) A total of 492 of Big Red Boat II's crew members were left stranded on Staten Island for several weeks as lawyers sorted out the financial quagmire.

Several years before the Disney-Premier partnership ran out in 1994, Disney CEO Michael Eisner was already thinking outside the box and told his chief lieutenants that he wanted to pull out of the Premier deal. That began a years-long process, trying to figure out just what course to take when it came to the Walt Disney Company's seaworthiness. For most of 1992, Disney explored three options: partnerships with two major cruise lines were on the table, as was the possibility of taking the bold move of starting its own cruise line. The final option—letting the Premier partnership run and getting out of cruising altogether—was a third possibility.

Eisner gathered some of his top executives in November of 1992 to tackle the cruise dilemma. In a meeting room in Glendale, California, were Eisner, Frank Wells, Al Weiss, and Frank Ioppolo. Larry Murphy, then the company's executive vice president and chief strategic officer, gave a comprehensive presentation on why Disney should go full speed ahead and commit to becoming a major player in the cruise industry. The executives loved the idea and the Disney Cruise Line, which would start with two yet-to-be-built ocean liners, was born.

Following the *Disney Magic*'s debut in 1998, the *Disney Wonder* joined DCL and also began sailing out of Disney's home port in Port Canaveral, Florida. In 2011 and 2012, DCL added two larger ships to the fleet: the *Disney Dream* and the *Disney Fantasy*. Plans are in the works to add three new ships to the line between 2021 and 2023. All three ships, to be built in Germany at the Meyer Werft Shipyards, will be bigger (they'll have 1,250 cabins, as compared to the *Magic* and *Wonder*'s 877 cabins). In addition, the three new ships will be powered by cleaner-burning liquified natural gas.

Earning My Wings

I don't think there are too many people
That are as lucky as me,
I have the most wonderful job
That there could ever be.

It's really quite rewarding
To lend a helping hand,
To a mom who's trying to take
All her children to Disneyland.

Not only do I get to travel to places far away,
At the end of each month, I earn a decent pay.

Nothing could ever make me happier
Then earning my wings every day.

(Colleen was an employee of Eastern Airlines from 1965 until 1981)

WALT DISNEY WORLD AND CORPORATE SPONSORSHIPS

Since the early days of Disneyland, corporate sponsorships have been an integral part of the Disney game plan. It was Walt Disney himself who realized early on that "no one company can do this by itself."

From a business standpoint, partnering with a successful company was a win-win for all parties involved. On opening day at Disneyland on July 17, 1955, guests saw a number of familiar nameplates as they strolled along Main Street, U.S.A., including Carnation, Upjohn, Maxwell House, and the Bank of America. Other corporations who sponsored attractions during Disneyland's early days included American Motors, Bell Systems, AT&T, and Monsanto.

The strategy of corporate sponsorship continued at the 1964–1965 New York World's Fair, where Disney developed four attractions. Three of the shows were sponsored by companies, while the fourth was paid for by the state of Illinois. Indeed, the four shows—Ford's Magic Skyway, General Electric's Carousel of Progress, Pepsi-Cola's "it's a small world," and the Illinois state pavilion's Great Moments with Mr. Lincoln—were among the biggest draws at the fair. Not only was the tab for creating the attractions picked up by the sponsors, but Walt Disney had written into the contracts that Disney owned the attractions and after the fair closed, each company would foot the bill for shipping their attractions across the country to Disneyland.

When Walt Disney World opened in 1971, companies flocked to Disney in hopes of having their corporate logos splashed on attractions and literature associated with the resort. GAF, for example, became the park's official photo company. In fact, GAF even provided the park's brochures, which included pages of photo-taking tips.

Another prominent corporate sponsor in 1971 was Eastern Airlines, which became known as the official airline of Walt Disney World. In addition to flying guests to Orlando International Airport, Eastern also sponsored an attraction in the Tomorrowland section of the park called If You Had Wings, a two-person Omnimover dark ride that promoted travel destinations throughout the Caribbean and elsewhere, all of which were, in keeping with the ride's sponsorship, serviced by Eastern. The ride had a catchy theme song, written by Disney composer Buddy Baker.

Shortly before Eastern's demise in 1989, Disney struck a deal with Delta Airlines, which not only became the new "official airline" of Walt Disney World, but also picked up sponsorship of the Tomorrowland attraction, renaming it Delta Dreamflight. Although the storyline changed to feature Delta's most glamorous destinations, the attraction still used the original Omnimover ride system.

In 1998, Delta Dreamflight was replaced by a new, cutting-edge attraction called Buzz Lightyear's Space Ranger Spin, where guests amassed points using a laser gun to shoot at targets emblazoned with Emperor Zurg's logo.

Corporate sponsorship played a huge role in the development of Epcot. According to Marty Sklar, former head of Walt Disney Imagineering, "These projects are so expensive. Without the sponsors, particularly in those days, you couldn't do those kinds of things. Disney didn't have the wherewithal to finance something like that by itself." Since Epcot cost an estimated $1.4 billion to build, that assessment was on the mark.

Once Disney CEO Card Walker gave the go-ahead to build Epcot, it was Sklar and a small band of Disney executives (among them Donn Tatum, Dick Nunis, and Jack Lindquist) who were charged with first finding out what Epcot would be, then finding leading companies in American industry to sponsor that vision. Disney reached out to several major companies through exploratory conferences. One company in particular, General Motors, seemed very interested in Epcot, which had now been distilled into a two-pronged project—one showcasing a variety of countries in a world's fair-type setting, the other touting the achievements and advancements of American industry.

After giving the executives at General Motors a detailed presentation, GM was on board. "They became the first ones to sign a contract at the end of 1978," Sklar said, and from that point on, companies seemed eager to be part of this exciting Epcot project. "That broke the dam, if you will, and Exxon was right behind them," Sklar continued. In rapid order, Bell System, Kodak, Kraft, General Electric, American Express, and Coca-Cola jumped at the opportunity to have their names associated with Epcot.

"There were a lot of visionaries in the companies that we dealt with who rolled the dice with us," Sklar said.

Hidden Mickeys

Hidden Mickeys are not so easy to spot,
So, when I see one, it truly warms my heart.
Start looking as soon as you enter Epcot's gate,
They're just about anywhere you ride or wait.
They can be located on a decorated door,
A ceiling, wall, or a beautiful floor.
You'll find Hidden Mickeys in the skies,
And supported by Viking warriors in disguise.
Discover all the Hidden Mickeys that you can spot,
I don't know how many there are, but it's certainly a lot.

THE STORY OF HIDDEN MICKEYS

Disney's Imagineers, the company's creative staff charged with dreaming up new and exciting attractions and adventures, have always been known to possess a sharp, not-so-subtle sense of humor. They're famous for poking fun at themselves or their fellow designers. They're also famous for putting hidden images into seemingly innocuous spaces, just for the heck of it.

One of those images, the Hidden Mickey, is anything that resembles the shape of Mickey Mouse's head: a rounded face with two smaller ears.

When the Imagineers were designing Epcot in the late 1970s, it was decided that the park would be aimed at an adult audience, with Disney characters kept to the Magic Kingdom. Nonetheless, they began incorporating Mickey Mouse-shaped images into a variety of design elements—wallpaper, rugs, paintings, and attraction props—as a way to keep the Mouse in the house. After receiving negative comments about the lack of characters in Epcot, Disney relented and Mickey, Minnie, Pluto, and

Goofy, dressed in futuristic garb, were added to the park. But the ever-clever Imagineers took the concept of their Hidden Mickeys and ran with it, placing them in just about everything they designed going forward.

In 1989, an article in *Eyes and Ears*, a newsletter for Walt Disney World cast members, was devoted to the unheard-of world of Hidden Mickeys, with a guide as to where to find many of them in the parks and resorts. The cat—make that the Mouse—was out of the bag. A few months later, *Disney News* picked up the story and a worldwide phenomenon was launched. Guests waiting in long queues would occupy themselves by seeking out anything that remotely resembled a Hidden Mickey. And guests staying in a Disney resort would find them hidden in plain sight, like on bed covers or embedded in the carpeting.

Over the years, the Hidden Mickey craze has remained constant, fueled in part by the flood of new images cleverly placed in new attractions and even on Disney Cruise Line's four ships.

Riding the PeopleMover

When the day is long and I'm really tired,
And rest time is required,
I travel inside and outside
On a most relaxing ride.
Relishing 10 minutes of rest,
While I remove all my stress.
I'm soon ready for new endeavor,
Enjoying my best day ever.

THE PEOPLEMOVER WAS PROPOSED BY WALT DISNEY HIMSELF

The Tomorrowland Transit Authority PeopleMover in the Magic Kingdom at Walt Disney World is an attraction that Walt Disney himself first proposed in the 1950s.

"Walt had long wanted some kind of overhead slow transportation system [at Disneyland] which could be built for use in cities as sort of a fast-walking overview" of what was below, said Bob Gurr, the Imagineer tasked with designing the PeopleMover as part of a Tomorrowland re-design in the mid-1960s.

Once completed and fully operational, Walt hoped the PeopleMover technology at Disneyland would serve as a working model and would subsequently find a place in cities, airports, and shopping malls as an efficient way to get people from Point A to Point B. Also in the back of Walt's mind was a prototype city of the future, where he envisioned clean-running PeopleMovers and monorails as the main modes of transportation for inhabitants, not noisy, exhaust-spewing cars, trucks, or buses. Indeed, early sketches of Epcot done by Imagineer Herb Ryman show PeopleMovers and monorails in abundance.

The genesis of the PeopleMover concept was designed by Gurr for the Ford Magic Skyway attraction at the 1964–1965 New York World's Fair. He came up with a system where a series of motors were placed in a track bed; each motor would rotate and when it came in contact with a plate at the bottom of each Ford Motor Company car, the motors would propel the cars forward. A few years later, a similar system was devised for the PeopleMover.

Disney mechanical engineer Bill Watkins "developed a track-mounted, drive-wheel propulsion system based on my successful Magic Skyway drive system," Gurr said.

From 1967 through 1995, the WEDway PeopleMover was an integral part of Disneyland's Tomorrowland landscape, as recognizable as the TWA Rocket, which was there on opening day in 1955, and Space Mountain. The PeopleMover was replaced by a short-lived attraction called Rocket Rods, which quickly faded into Disney parks lore. Curiously, the dormant PeopleMover track bed remains in place to this day.

The WEDway PeopleMover in the Magic Kingdom at Walt Disney World opened in 1975. It remains in operation to this day, though it was renamed the Tomorrowland Transit Authority PeopleMover as part of a new Tomorrowland makeover in 2010.

Guests often confuse PeopleMover technology to the Omnimover system, which Gurr also had a hand in developing.

There are key differences between the PeopleMover and the Omnimover systems. "The Omnimover is a connected endless chain of vehicles," Gurr said. "The Haunted Mansion is an Omnimover."

On the Omnimover system, the ride vehicles have the ability to twist and turn and go up and down inclines; on a PeopleMover system, the vehicles travel straight ahead on a flat track, with the ability to negotiate turns.

Grandma Knows Best

Advice from a Disney mom is rather important,
They give travelers suggestions and reinforcement.

But lessons from a Disney grandma are important, too,
This Disney grandma has several secrets for you.

Old people never like to spend time waiting in line,
If it's busy, get FastPass and come back another time.

If you can afford it, never ever stay off-site,
Stay on property and enjoy a full day and night.

Every time you visit a quick-service food location,
Tell the server Grandma needs free water for medication.

Hotel guests can take the monorail or buses all day,
You'll see new sights and save money on a rainy day.

The next time you see Cinderella or Princess Aurora,
Ask cast members to take pictures with your camera.

Old people know how to save lots of time and money,
We know the best ways to spend our days, rainy or sunny.

Finding Lost Parents

Kids don't get lost inside Disney parks,
But every now and then, grownups do
Always take daily photos with your group,
So, if you become lost, it's easier to find you.
Cast members will soon be on the lookout,
For adults that look exactly like you.
They'll know what you are wearing,
A dark green shirt or perhaps powder blue.
And before you can say Mickey Mouse,
You'll be reunited with your entire crew.

A WORLD OF AMENITIES IS AVAILABLE TO DISNEY GUESTS

A day at Walt Disney World or Disneyland can be filled with fun, excitement, and thrills. But on those rare occasions when things don't go exactly as planned, the skilled Disney cast members are trained to respond to just about any situation, including family members who are lost.

There also are myriad of amenities available to guests to help make their visit as enjoyable as possible.

It starts at the entrance of each park, where wheelchair and stroller rentals are available. Nearby, lockers may be rented to store any of your excess gear.

Throughout each park, guests will find handicap-accessible restrooms, as well as companion facilities. There are designated parade viewing areas for guests with disabilities, as well as devices available at Guest Relations which offer assistive listening, handheld captioning, video captioning, and audio description.

Moms with young children can take advantage of baby care centers in each park, where you and your young one can bask in comfort and care while in a cool, quiet setting.

For those guests bringing service dogs into a park, there are specially designated relief areas for the canines.

When it comes to medical issues, the four parks at Walt Disney World and the two at Disneyland have numerous automated external defibrillators (AED) clearly marked and scattered throughout the parks. In addition, each park has a first-aid station where guests can receive care for minor injuries.

In need of some extra cash for shopping? There are ATMs in each park. Lost the cap to your camera? There's a lost-and-found located near the entrance of each park.

Lastly, if you become separated from your family, alert any Disney cast member or make your way to Guest Relations, where they'll be happy to assist you in re-uniting with your group.

Disney Days with Grandma

Visiting Disney with Grandma was as wonderful as could be,
As we entered each Epcot pavilion she explained family history.

She said Grandpa is Norwegian then she took my picture on
top of a giant troll,
And she bought a Mommy book about bridges in Norway
with a very special toll.

My great-great-grandma was born in Germany, so we
stopped there for a bite
Grandma said we could buy Daddy an Italian sweatshirt tonight.

In Scotland we bought a tile with Great-Grandpa's coat of arms,
When we saw an Irish cottage, Grandma told me about her
family's farms.

When I return to school and my teacher asks what I did on
my vacation,
I'll proudly tell her I learned about my family history and
visited each location.

About the Authors

After Colleen Ann Myrhol married her high school sweetheart, Lenny, they dove into a life-long love affair... with Disney.

They are retired airline employees and together they have traveled to 48 states, 91 countries, six continents, and one truly Magical Kingdom. In fact, they went to Disneyland on their honeymoon and Disneyland Paris to celebrate their 25th wedding anniversary.

Now that Colleen uses a wheelchair, it is easier for her to travel the world on the Disney Cruise Line (DCL). Colleen and Lenny, along with their friends and fellow Disney Vacation Club members and native Staten Islanders Hank and Ginny Osborne, have sailed with DCL to North and South America, Europe, and Africa.

Colleen started writing poetry at age 11 when her grammar school English teacher urged his students to enter a public-television poetry contest. Colleen won the contest, and was hooked. It became a wonderful way for her to make a journal of her worldwide travels. After she began her second career, she all but stopped writing poetry until years later. Colleen has multiple sclerosis (MS) and her doctors and fellow poets at the Staten Island MS Center suggested she resume her poetry as a way to help her cognitive ability and to overcome the brain damage caused by MS. She hopes to encourage others with MS, low vision, and cognitive issues to pick up a pen and spread their wings with poetry.

CHUCK SCHMIDT was bitten by the Disney bug at an early age. He remembers watching *The Mickey Mouse Club* on TV after school in the mid-1950s and *Walt Disney's Wonderful World of Color* on Sunday nights. During his 48-year career in the newspaper business, he channeled that love of Disney as the Sunday News and Travel editor for the *Staten Island Advance*, writing features and covering a variety of events involving the expansive world created by Walt Disney.

Disney in Verse is his fifth book published by Theme Park Press. The others are *Disney's Animal Kingdom: An Unofficial History*, *On the Disney Beat*, *An American in Disneyland Paris*, and *Disney's Dream Weavers*. He also collaborated with former Disney cast member Ted Kellogg on his book, *Passport to Pixie Dust*.

Since 2009, Chuck has shared his passion for all things Disney in his *Goofy About Disney* blog on SILive.com. He also writes a blog for AllEars.net called *Still Goofy About Disney*.

Chuck resides in Beachwood, New Jersey, with his wife, Janet. They have three adult children and six grandchildren.

ABOUT THEME PARK PRESS

Theme Park Press publishes books primarily about the Disney company, its history, culture, films, animation, and theme parks, as well as theme parks in general.

Our authors include noted historians, animators, Imagineers, and experts in the theme park industry.

We also publish many books by first-time authors, with topics ranging from fiction to theme park guides.

And we're always looking for new talent. If you'd like to write for us, or if you're interested in the many other titles in our catalog, please visit:

www.ThemeParkPress.com

● ●

Theme Park Press Newsletter

Subscribe to our free email newsletter and enjoy:

- ◆ Free book downloads and giveaways
- ◆ Access to excerpts from our many books
- ◆ Announcements of forthcoming releases
- ◆ Exclusive additional content and chapters
- ◆ And more good stuff available nowhere else

To subscribe, visit www.ThemeParkPress.com, or send email to newsletter@themeparkpress.com.

Read more about these books
and our many other titles at:

www.ThemeParkPress.com

32106215R00091

Made in the USA
Middletown, DE
07 January 2019